# THE GOD SOLUTION

# THE GOD SOLUTION

*The Power of Pure Love*

# NEALE DONALD WALSCH

**PHOENIX BOOKS**

For licensing information please contact:
Phoenix Books, Inc.
369 So Beverly Drive, Suite 381
Beverly Hills, CA 90212-3807
(310) 273-7722
*info@phoenixbooksinc.com*

PUBLICATION HISTORY
ISBN: 978-1-73572-270-2 (Hardcover)
ISBN: 978-1-73572-273-3 (Audiobook)
ISBN: 978-1-73572-271-9 (mobi)
ISBN: 978-1-73572-272-6 (ePub)

Library of Congress Cataloguing-in-Publication Data Available

# PART I

## *A New Idea*

# 1

Let's say, for the sake of discussion, that humanity could *prove beyond a doubt* that God exists. Do you think that would affect your life in any way? Would it make a difference, as a practical matter?

Let's say, for the sake of discussion, that humanity could prove beyond a doubt that *God does not exist.* Do you think that would affect your life in any way? Would it make a difference, as a practical matter?

CRSO

A whole lot of people have explored those questions for a whole lot of time. Like, say, *billions* of people over *thousands of years.*

I think that makes it fair to consider that questions about God are neither trivial nor irrelevant. Much depends on what is being said on this subject.

If the Pope were to declare tomorrow, for instance, that he was wrong about everything and that there's no such thing as God, the emotional underpinnings of a huge swath of our species would be shaken to the core.

If the spiritual leaders of all the other world religions were to say they agreed with him, the spiritual lives of *8/10ths of the human race* would be in shambles.

Surveys show that nearly 85% of the world's people identify with a religious group and believe in a controlling power.

Yet…the world is a mess.

*So, what difference does it make whether God exists or not?*

CRISO

There comes a moment in every species' development when timidity no longer serves, when more than the proverbial lone voice in the wilderness cries out to be heard; when it's Fair Question Time.

As a devastating global virus, as devastating racial injustice, and as devastating economic collapse assailed the planet in 2020, the Fair Question is: If a benevolent Higher Power exists, what's the *problem* here? Why is life on Earth not any better?

Perhaps it's presumptuous to suggest an answer, and one hates to sound simplistic, but could the problem be that we simply haven't found a way to *engage with* that Higher Power, if it does exist?

Humanity can't seem to come to a collective agreement about who and what God *is,* what God wants, what God does, and how God does it.

There's a huge irony here. Do you see the irony? Eight out of ten of us *agree about* a Higher Power *we can't agree about.*

We agree that It exists, but that's the beginning and the end of it. About everything else, we're all over the map. One religion declares this, one religion declares that. One culture says this, one culture says that. One person claims this, one person claims that.

Do we listen to the Priest, to the Imam, to the Rabbi, to the Minister? Do we heed the words of the Priestess, of the

Preacher, of the Pastor, of the Monk? Do we follow the example of the Sister, of the Brother, of others in Holy Orders?

Could it be that what each of them is so sure is true is all just wishful thinking, and that there is no "God"? Or...

...OR...

...*could what we say we know about God simply be inaccurate?*

This is what I have come to call the God Dilemma.

ॐ

Does any of this matter? I think it does. In fact, I know it does. It matters because it's rendered us singularly incapable of bringing to bear the power of the God we say we *believe* in, as a means of building the world we say we want to *live* in.

But now there's hope. Because enough people like you are asking enough questions like this, we have enough of a chance to turn enough of this around to make enough of life work at last.

We can produce an answer to this dilemma. We can embrace The God Solution.

Oh, and by the way, this is not what most people encountering those three words might think that it is.

# 2

Let's start by agreeing that what human beings believe about God and about life is important.

Some people say that our ideas about all of this are nothing but mental exercises, at best, and that we need to get on with what really matters. That may sound all well and good, except that what really matters *arises* out of what we believe.

Looking deeply at this reveals the following: beliefs create behaviors, behaviors create experience, experience creates reality. And the realities we've created out of our belief about God and about life do not paint a pretty picture.

We're talking about a species that permits 1.7 billion of its members to go their entire lives without a drop of clean water; that seems not to be bothered by the fact that 1.6 billion still do not have electricity; that looks the other way as 2.6 billion exist without indoor toilets; that allows over 650 of its children to die of starvation every *hour*.

There has been armed conflict somewhere on this planet for 92% of recorded history. One member of our species commits suicide every 40 seconds. In 2017, just under 465,000 of us were murdered. Add the numbers in these statistics and you get a pretty good idea of how well our species is doing as a civilization.

And if you think our ideas about God have little to do with all of this, think again. 80% of civil law in most of the countries of Europe and the West is based on Canon Law. In other words, the teachings *of a religion.*

Then there are our day-to-day cultural behaviors, the decisions and the choices we make. These, too, are based on our most sacred beliefs about who we are in relation to each other, and about how life should work.

The result: even the people who are not part of the statistics I've presented here are too often unhappy. Folks are struggling. Many are feeling unsettled and are experiencing turmoil in their day-to-day lives. Too many, in fact, for a society that tells itself it is an Advanced Civilization.

Nobody wants it this way. Most humans deeply desire peace, security, opportunity, sufficiency, stability, and all the health, happiness, joy and love we can jam into a lifetime. Yet we seem utterly unable to produce these outcomes on a consistent basis for any but the tiniest percentage of us.

And it's not as if we just started trying last week. *We've been trying for 50 millennia.* Without success.

Is anybody asking why? Or more to the point, *Why* isn't anybody asking why? Perhaps we're afraid to question the basic beliefs that undergird our spiritual understandings. Or maybe we're afraid to have anyone *hear* us questioning those beliefs.

CRSO

Humanity's biggest dilemma relating to God is not whether people think there *is* or *is not* a God, but what those who think there *is* a God hold as their belief *about* God.

If we really are an Advanced Civilization—as in capital A, capital C—why *is*...truly, *why is*...life on Earth the way it is?

And if we are not as advanced as we imagine we are, is there anything, *anything*, we could do to accelerate our progress as a species, and as an individual member *of* that species?

Yes.

We could come up with one totally clear, overarching, *and commonly held* belief about the Higher Power.

Such a belief could unite humanity within the framework of *a single theological, philosophical and emotional ethic*—and this could be extraordinarily powerful in ending our collectively dysfunctional and mutually self-destructive behaviors.

Agreeing on a jointly embraced statement about God can't be that difficult, and it couldn't be more urgent, given the direction in which our world is heading.

What's interesting is that thousands of humans share thousands of commonly held beliefs about thousands of other things. We've come to conclusions on some of the biggest mysteries our tribe has encountered. Yet with all of our genius, all of our ingenuity, all of our intelligence, and in spite of all of our evolutionary advancement, we can't seem to come even *close* to producing a commonly held belief about the most important aspect of life of all.

Is the truth about this really that unknowable? Is it accurate to say that "mysterious are the ways of the Lord"?

I don't think so. We've certainly *experienced* them as unknowable, but that's not because it's impossible to know more about them. Rather, it's because we haven't sought to do so with our minds open, rather than closed. With our hearts connected, rather than disconnected. With the voice of our souls amplified by a common desire, rather than muffled by our collective fear of unacceptable and unallowable answers.

The good news is that we have, after 50 millennia, finally reached the point in our evolution where we are just one step away from *solving* the God Dilemma.

The bad news is that the solution may require us to challenge, and maybe even (hold your breath) *change,* some of our most sacred beliefs, which we've clung to for a long, long time.

# 3

Changing beliefs is not something that human beings do easily or quickly.

It took the Catholic Church 359 years to admit that Galileo Galilei was right when he dared to propose that our planet was not the center of the universe as the Church taught, and to reverse its excommunication of him. But humanity finally came to its senses.

It took the medical profession over half a century to admit that Hungarian physician Ignaz Semmelweis was right in 1847 when he dared to propose that if doctors sterilized their hands with disinfectant before going from one medical procedure to the next, patient infections (and infant mortalities) would be greatly reduced, and that we need to reverse our blindness to the existence of germs. But humanity finally came to its senses.

The amazing work that has been done in mapping the human genome would not have been possible were it not for Barbara McClintock, whose work as a geneticist was initially unaccepted by the scientific community, which told her that her discovery of the existence of jumping genes—sequences of DNA that move between the genome—was nothing more than "junk DNA". In 1983 she was awarded a Nobel Prize as the significance of her work was recognized. Humanity came to its senses after realizing that she had been "right" about what everyone said she was "wrong" about.

CRE

This list could go on, this naming of Those Who Had It Wrong— and who we eventually honored as Those Who Had It Right. I've come up with my own way of describing the people on this list. I call them Idea Heroes.

The dictionary defines heroism as "great bravery," and I think it takes great bravery to make a public pronouncement of something about which one knows ahead of time that hundreds, perhaps thousands (and maybe even millions) will disagree.

It's thanks to Idea Heroes that most of us finally agree that germs exist, that jumping genes exist, and that a great many other things we once did not believe to be true are, as it turns out, true as True Can Be.

But what is true about God? Ah, back to the dilemma again. The challenge in reaching consensus here is that there's more than one question on the table, and this is what has created such difficulty for our species in coming to a collective agreement.

There's not only the question of whether there *is* a Higher Power, but—if it does exist—what that Higher Power consists of. What is Its essential nature? What are Its attributes, Its defining properties, Its characteristics? What is Its desire? Does It even *have* desires? What is Its usefulness? Can It even *be* "used"?

# 4

Will asking questions about God *one more time* do nothing but invite more intellectual excursions that in the end take us to exactly where we are right now? Will we still be a world divided and undecided about a Higher Power—and about just about everything else?

The answer is yes, if we're going to allow ourselves to be satisfied with the same answers we've come up with before. But what if we came up with *different* answers, *daring* answers? And what if we invited ourselves to do that deliberately?

This is precisely how science has produced amazing discoveries. This is how medicine has produced miraculous cures. This is how technology has produced incredible inventions. Is there a reason we have decided this is a *sin*—perhaps the *highest* offense—when it comes to theology?

The word "theology" is defined as the *study* of God, not as the one and only, firm and final truth about God. So, we would do well to study this further. Why did certain people in religious communities become theologians if they felt there was no more to know or to explain about God?

We notice that people such as Francis of Assisi, Catherine of Siena, Thomas Aquinas, Martin Buber, Hildegard of Bingen, Ibn

Arabi, Julian of Norwich, Judith Plaskow, African theologians Bolaji Idowu, John Mbiti, and Kwesi Dickson, and many others of many traditions have felt that there was more to study and more to say about God.

What if *we* became theologians and began our own deep look to see if there could be an as-yet-not-widely-held understanding of the term "Higher Power"? What if this could clarify everything?

Is humanity even available to such a possibility? Or are we so closed-minded that even a suggestion that we permit an exploration of the highest truth to venture outside The Boundary of the Orthodox is not to be tolerated?

Is this what we have come to?

I'm going to suggest that this is *not* who we are, but that the *limitations we've placed on our thinking* have produced an aberration. I propose that coming up with a single, overarching understanding about God could be the best thing that humanity ever did for itself.

For those who today believe in a Higher Power, for those who today do not believe in a Higher Power, and for those who on this day aren't sure one way or the other, I predict that the benefit would be equal. But what we need now are some Idea Heroes.

Might you be one of them?

CRSO

Idea Heroes are not just those who come up with revolutionary—and in some places totally unacceptable—ideas, but also those who are willing to *listen* to new ideas from others and explore them fully.

Idea Heroes have the bravery to allow some of their preconceived notions to be challenged—especially long-standing ideas about God and Life and Each Other.

Idea Heroes possess the courage to cross the Border Of Certainties to explore the Territory Of Possibilities.

I think it's important—*very* important—for us to do that today.

Why? Because if there *is* a Higher Power, and we're simply not using it effectively, wouldn't that be a shame? Wouldn't it be a terrible waste?

# 5

I'm going to be a little unorthodox here and stray from the way books are normally written, because something happened in the middle of producing this one that shifted the entire direction of the narrative.

My wife Em came into the room as I was putting this chapter together and said something that stopped me cold. She knew, of course, what I was working on, as we'd had discussions about it. And she said as she stepped in:

"I just had a thought. *What if each of us could create our own religion? What would our religion look like? And what would it look like if everyone else followed that religion?*"

I wound up staring out the window for ten minutes after that. What an intriguing idea. What a table-turning-over idea.

If you were Chief Operating Officer of the Universe and you could have your way, what would your way be?

What would your religion teach? What would be its organizing principles? And what do you think it would look like if everyone in the world followed your religion?

Okay now, just enjoy this. Don't let it tax you, just let it intrigue you. If you started your own religion, how would you answer the most common questions people have about a Higher

Power? What *would* be Its essential nature and Its desire? What *would* be Its usefulness?

CRSO

While you're giving this a little thought, let me share with you that I think it's possible for all of us to agree on a single, culture-spanning idea about God which *the whole of humanity* could embrace.

I think that a decision to embrace such an idea (an idea that I call The God Solution) would be that one final step I spoke of earlier that will raise us to the level of a truly Advanced Civilization.

The idea itself? The single concept or declaration that could be embraced by people of every culture, everywhere on the planet?

Now *that* might be a little harder to guess.

Shall we hypothesize?

# 6

 In support of a continuing exploration in the Territory of Possibilities, I'm going to work on the assumption that a Higher Power does exist. I'm clear that this is not an assumption with which everyone agrees, but it's a "hypothetical" that allows the exploration to move forward—much as a scientist might embrace an unproven assumption as part of initiating an experiment.

With nearly 85% of humans believing that a Higher Power exists, it seems like it a fair place to start in search of a single, unifying concept, ethic, or declaration of principle that would serve the world entire. I'm going to suggest again that the reason our world is so filled with problems, suffering, turmoil and unhappiness is that we just haven't been able to rally around such a concept. *We simply can't seem to come to a collective agreement about the Higher Power that would allow us to make effective use of it.*

That, in a sentence, is the God Dilemma. And the chief *reason* we can't reach agreement is that the majority of humans simply aren't clear about what the Higher Power is, or how it works.

To be fair, this is completely understandable. Not many folks have taken a course in Comprehensive Theology, enrolled in a class in Practical Metaphysics, or attended a graduate school for Applied Energetics.

But what if we don't need such a course, such a class, or such a school? What if we each only need to listen to our heart? If we did that, I predict we would all decide that God is nothing more mysterious than — dare I suggest it? — Pure Love.

I find myself wanting to say that anyone and everyone who has ever experienced what they feel has been a direct connection with the energy of The Divine knows exactly what I am talking about. I think they would not disagree that God *is*, in a phrase, Pure Love.

I'm suggesting here that what most people call "God" is not a bigger-than-life "person," but rather, a self-conscious, self-aware, self-sourcing energy that can and does take any physical form It wishes. It can appear to be an entity just like us (or any other sentient being in the universe), but It is much more, much larger, than that. And when the energy I've just described is projected through or by any one of us, it can be *felt*.

With that as my framework, I'll be using the word "God" on these pages as shorthand for this energetic expression. So please consider the words God, Pure Love, Higher Power, and Energy as being interchangeable here.

I want to now propose that Pure Love is the most game-changing, impactful, and effective creative force in the universe.

Now I think it's fair game if some would say: *"Really? Is that all that this 'intellectual excursion' is going to offer us? Is that the extent of the so-called 'new answer' we've been dared to come up with here? God is pure love? Wow, big revelation."*

But wait. There is more here than may meet the eye.

It's all hypothesis, for sure, but what if—like other ideas that were initially dismissed because they were said to be All Wrong—this idea turns out to be All Right?

Might that finally make things all right between all people in our world?

CRSO

Love is a simple, even humble word we've used on this planet to describe what may not be such a simple, humble energy. I'm going to suggest that it's a particular *kind* of energy that may be more powerful than we have fully realized.

Through the centuries, the use of love has too often been seen to be too simplistic or too naïve to have any real value as a *creative force*. It might make us feel better, but it doesn't help us create better. Unless...

...unless there really *is* more here than meets the eye; more than the simple sharing or expression of gentle feelings. Unless Pure love is an *energy*. Not just a nice idea, a sweet thought, but the words that we use in human language to refer to an *energetic projection* with a vibration so specific, so particular, and so powerful that it impacts and affects other energy configurations in ways that can often significantly alter them. Not unlike pouring warm water over an ice cube.

# 7

I'm offering as a conjecture that the words Pure Love are as close as any words in Earth's languages can come to describing the Signature Vibration of the Cosmos, and how it *feels*. If that is so, we could then use the phrase "God is Pure Love" to put this description into one short sentence describing the Deity.

Could *this* be the jointly-held single notion that virtually every person who believes in God could easily embrace? And could the power of us *jointly* embracing it produce an enormously positive expansive energetic, and thus, a remarkable impact on our world?

*Just a second, just a second,* some might say. *We already* do *jointly hold this idea. There's hardly a person in the world who would not agree that God is Love. That's the Big Revelation???*

Well, yes and no. Many wonderful teachers and messengers through the years have placed that truth before us. Marianne Williamson's wonderful book *A Return to Love* is a brilliant example.

The "big revelation" I am offering would be that God is *Pure* Love. I'm persisting in putting those two words together, because that's a particular *kind* of love which wants and needs nothing in return.

Now, can we believe in a Higher Power such as *this*? Is this *The God Solution?* And if we accept this idea about God, can we then use it to form a *global ethic* that we apply to our day-to-day political, economic, social, and spiritual interactions on Earth?

I say that we can. I know that we're entirely capable, as individuals and as a species, of using Pure Love as our Gold Standard when making decisions about how we choose to behave and what we seek to create on our planet.

The solution to the God Dilemma can be easier than we may think. It can be as easy as asking, at critical junctures in our decision-making, a simple question: *Does it feel like Pure Love is being expressed?*

CRSO

The challenge will be that people have chosen to *define* Pure Love in many different ways. For instance…

…when we hear of a man being strapped into a chair and having 2,000 volts of electricity run through his body as punishment for what he has done, *Does it feel like Pure Love is being expressed?*

When we hear that some people are not allowed to vote, not allowed to drive, not allowed to attend school, or not allowed to hold a particular job, because they are not male, *Does it feel like Pure Love is being expressed?*

When we hear that rental of an apartment, or the purchase of a wedding cake, or the issuing of a marriage license, has been refused to a couple because they are the same sex, *Does it feel like Pure Love is being expressed?*

Now there are some people who would say *yes* to some of those questions. They would say that it is their Pure Love of *God* that has motivated those actions. In fact, there are those who would say that God has *ordered* these things.

So we confront a glaring paradox. We see that what some people say God has ordered is not at all the same as what some people say that God's own *son* has recommended. He called it the Golden Rule.

And what if the new *collective agreement* of our species was for us to actually *live* the Golden Rule, and do unto others only what we would want done to us? Could that work?

We don't know. We've never tried it. It may be the Golden *Rule*, but we've apparently decided that it is not going to be the Gold *Standard* for our own behavior.

# 8.

There is a reason that we have been astonishingly unable to create peace, security, opportunity, sufficiency, stability, and all the health, happiness, joy and love we can jam into a lifetime for more than a tiny percentage of humanity.

*Could it be that we are missing the central ingredient?*

What I am proposing here is that it would serve us to explore more deeply the tool that is the feeling called Pure Love.

I'll go further. I will suggest that we actually create a brand-new definition of God.

Let me highlight that, because it could be easy for you to just pass over as you move through your reading here. It *begs* to be highlighted, because it was not a small suggestion, not a run-of-the-mill proposal. I believe that it is, in fact, that one step I've been talking about which could elevate our entire civilization. So...the suggestion again?

**Create a brand-new definition of God.**

I am inviting us to define God as the feeling called Pure Love.

I realize that this is putting things into the simplest terms, but perhaps that's exactly what's been needed. This could be just short of revolutionary. Or, at the very least, novel and far-reaching.

Some people would describe God as an Entity; a super wise, incredibly powerful, ever present entity. Some others might define the Higher Power as an energy that had sourced, and continues to source, All That Is. But most people do not usually say, "God is a feeling."

They may say that God *creates* feelings, or that an experience of God *produces* a wonderful feeling, but it is not generally said or taught that what God *is,* is a feeling itself. Yet if we decided to all be Idea Heroes and give ourselves permission to propose that God is Pure Love (not simply love, but Pure Love—and there is a huge difference, which is what makes this definition spiritually revolutionary), we might just *eliminate the division* between people who believe that God exists and those who say that God does not. Virtually everyone on Earth would agree that Pure Love exists.

Surely most mothers experience Pure Love for their newborn. When they cradle that baby in their arms, they love purely, with no need for one single thing in return.

Surely most people experience Pure Love if and when they find themselves at the bedside of a dying parent. Or spouse. Or child. When they hold the hand of their loved one, they have no need for *one single thing* in return.

To move to a lighter example, I have witnessed people experience Pure Love when they're petting an animal. They want and need nothing in return.

Perhaps you've expressed this kind of love in your life. Perhaps you've received it from another.

True, a few might say they've never experienced it, but almost everyone would acknowledge that it exists. Indeed, it's because they've seen it expressed by others that many yearn to experience it themselves.

Maybe we *have,* in the explorations here, accidentally come up with what could easily and quickly become humanity's Common Denominator, an overarching, *collectively held* idea of God that the entire species can embrace.

What do you think? Is this definition of God too simple to actually be applied?

Things get complicated, for sure, when we consider, as has been noted here, that many people have thought of Pure Love in many different ways. So I see that, if I'm going to suggest that we change our definition of God, then I need to be very clear, very precise regarding exactly what the words 'Pure Love' mean, what the total nuance is, as I employ the term. I'll use a few more words here.

To me, Pure Love means that in the expression of it, nothing is intended, expected, or needed as a return for the self. Pure Love is an act of selflessness. It is founded in the self's awareness that it requires and must demand nothing to be perfectly happy. It is a joyful outcome of the decision to continue its flow without ever having the intention of any negative outcome or energy experienced by the receiver. In this, it is the granting of total freedom to the recipient of this love to respond in any way they wish.

The delineation here is that when you love someone for the sheer beauty of the expression, for the sheer wonder of it, for the consummate joy of it—for the happiness it brings *you* to feel that energy glowing inside of you and sent out from you—then you are loving purely. If you are looking to get something back in return as your reward for sending love out, then you are not loving someone else, *you are loving yourself,* and simply using another as a means of doing it.

25

I now find myself wondering: If there is a God, how do you think it is that God loves?

# 9

My understanding is that it is from the energy I call God that our planet arose, and all the life forms on it. Likewise, the entire universe.

One can call this process "evolution" through "natural selection" if one wishes to, but evolutionism doesn't adequately address the matter of First Cause. In short, the fact that evolution as a process exists does not, *ipso facto,* mean that God does *not* exist. God could just as easily have used "evolution" as any other means with which to create the Universe.

And my idea is that this self-aware, self-conscious Source needs and asks nothing in return, having expressed Its energy in this way for the sheer joy of it. So, for me, the way that God loves is without strings attached. I mean, no strings *whatsoever.* No requirements, no "do-this-or-else" directives, no my-way-or-the-highway edicts.

It's just an idea I have. It makes me feel good to think of God in this way. I could be wrong about it all, but when I look at the night sky on a cloudless night and just take in the glittering canopy…and when I think of the thousands—nay, millions—of places where intelligent life must exist…I find it difficult to believe that the Originating Source wants and demands something in return from every single one of the trillions of sentient beings on those millions of glittering homes, and they must all meet those demands or spend their non-physical life in indescribable suffering forevermore.

If *humans* were running the place, I could see such a set up. But God? A Deity so magnificent as to have created the canopy I'm looking at, wants and commands something from me for placing me here—where I didn't even ask to be placed?

CRSO

This is really quite a breathtaking place, this sphere called Earth. It's eye-poppingly magnificent in its beauty, mind-bogglingly abundant with resources, heart-openingly welcoming to an evolving species. We could have a utopia here. All we have to do is care for each other, and for our home.

We've decided not to.

Caring for each other and for our planet is something we obviously need help with. It clearly doesn't come naturally to us yet, no doubt because we're just emerging from the earliest stages of our development as a species of sentient beings. Still, we're beginning to move in a new direction in our evolutionary process.

Some countries on Earth have actually stopped killing people intentionally as their means of teaching people that killing people intentionally is not okay. They've eliminated capital punishment—a device whose continued use had been justified by an Old Definition eye-for-an-eye idea of God—having decided that one of the most advanced minds among us (Albert Einstein) was on to something when he made the observation that a problem cannot be solved using the same energy that created it.

We've taken other steps, as well, that can move us toward becoming that more Advanced Civilization we spoke of earlier.

Some societies have actually decided that females should have the same rights and privileges as males. Some societies have actually declared that people who love each other should be able to marry each other, whatever their sexual orientation. Some societies have actually chosen to ignore the color of a person's skin in the application of its laws.

So we're getting there. We haven't "arrived" yet, but we're getting there. And our next step is to embrace The God Solution. We can do this by deciding anew and agreeing collectively about Who and What God Is and exploring together When and How this Higher Power works. Then we can approach our challenging and difficult human relationships from an entirely different perspective and make some of the problems we've created go away.

Maybe all of them.

Self-made problems should not be the bane of an Advanced Civilization. Advanced Civilizations move beyond that. The solution being proposed here—a New Definition Approach— is about more than redefining God as Pure Love. It's about a whole new way of living that *arises out* of this new definition.

You'll remember that I've said here that solving the God Dilemma may require us to challenge, and even to change, some pretty basic ideas that we may hold about God and about Life.

It will.

You may also recall that I said there is more here than may meet the eye in the idea of re-defining God as Pure Love.

There is.

You are now going to find on these pages an entirely different way of using the Higher Power that so many of us say must surely exist. It is an alternate way of approaching life. This is a

29

method to which many people may never have given serious consideration before.

This new way can change the world. Hypothetically, of course. We'd have to try it to see.

Want to do that? Want to give it a look, at least?

Ah, you *are* an Idea Hero.

# 10.

There's a new way to use the energetics of Thought and Emotion that can bring God as Pure Love into the picture powerfully and purposefully.

This new way involves swapping out one element for the other. It changes what has been a hallowed approach to personal growth and self-development; an approach that we've been encouraged to use for many years.

You may have noticed that most of the teaching on self-development has centered around changing our thinking. The word *feeling* is not mentioned nearly as often as the word *thought* when describing the mechanism by which metaphysics generates effects and outcomes in our physical world.

A man named James Allen produced a classic on this subject, a literary essay he titled *As a Man Thinketh*. It was published as a booklet in 1903 and has been standard reading in the self-improvement movement for over a hundred years.

I'm going to quote a write-up of it found at Amazon. com, because it illustrates exactly what I am now talking about regarding the most often recommended way to improve our lives. The write-up said that the work "was described by Allen as '…dealing with the power of thought, and particularly with the use and application of thought to happy and beautiful issues.'

"Allen has tried to make the book simple, so that all can easily grasp and follow its teaching and put into practice the methods which it advises. It shows how, in his own thought-world, each man holds the key to every condition, good or bad, that enters into his life, and that, by working patiently and intelligently upon his thoughts, he may remake his life, and transform his circumstances."

In short, the book is all about what Allen calls "the right application of thought". There are many other books on this subject as well, of course. Some of the better known in this genre include *The Power of Positive Thinking* by Rev. Dr. Norman Vincent Peale, *Psycho-Cybernetics* by Dr. Maxwell Maltz, *Think and Grow Rich* by Napoleon Hill, *The Magic of Thinking Big* by David J. Schwartz, and *Change Your Thoughts, Change Your Life* by Dr. Wayne Dyer.

I'm not going to suggest now that those books are not valuable. I read Mr. Allen's book 50 years ago and it changed my life. I read Dr. Peale's book and it sent me soaring. I knew Wayne Dyer personally, and he inspired me with his very presence in a room.

Many other people have found the writings I've mentioned above, and other books like them, to offer wonderful help in finding and using a tool with which to improve their lives. Yet what I am hoping you will notice again is that those texts focus mainly on the *thoughts* we most often entertain.

I'm making this point for a reason. I'm going to suggest here that it's the *emotions* we create *with* our thoughts that are more powerful tools than thoughts themselves, principally because emotions put thoughts into motion. Perhaps this is the point that other books sought to make, but I think much more attention could (and should) be directed to the emotions we choose as the first place we need to look. I observe that it's here where our most powerful creative force is born.

There's a difference, believe me. A person can have a thought and pay it very little attention—or even completely ignore it— deciding it is not necessary or not welcome. But once a person translates an idea (which is a relatively benign energetic vibration) into an emotion (which is a much more energetically condensed vibration), they produce an energetic sensation that creates far more impact in a person's body. And if the emotion is felt strongly enough, its energy projects into that person's exterior environment.

It is when people become emotional over what they have been thinking that their energy reverberates more widely.

This is not new information. Esther Hicks and her late husband, Jerry, pointed to the power of energy and vibration in their books, as have other authors. We are making a crystal-clear distinction between Thought and Emotion here because these pages contain a suggestion to take a New Definition Approach to understanding God. This approach identifies the Higher Power not simply as an amorphous energy, but as a particular and very specific *kind* of energy that generates an immediately identifiable *feeling*.

CRSO

You can see that I am not treating "energy" as a stand-alone subject here, but rather, as part of a larger overview that includes and, in fact, defines and expresses The Divine. I'm interested in a clear explanation of how we can *engage interactively* with the Higher Power in a two-way process of purposeful creation.

This process can supply the answer to the question, *What difference does it make if God exists or not?*

It's a fine-tuning of the Change-Your-Thoughts/Change-Your-Life method of self-improvement and personal development. Many books on this subject don't even mention the word "God."

I suggest that it's the fine-tuning which has been largely missing from humanity's evolutionary process, and that *this is why that process has stalled.*

Eight out of ten of us may agree that a Higher Power exists, but I'm betting that only two out of ten of us *use that power intentionally, consistently, and constructively.*

The result: our species is still acting like barbarians in many, many ways. We still have grown-ups who lead nations threatening grown-ups who lead nations, for heaven's sake. Groups continue to attack groups. Individuals keep hurting individuals. Lack of equality runs rampant in our collective life, and we not only allow it to, in many places and in many ways, we encourage it to. We can't seem to stop ourselves. As a collective, as a species, as a civilization, we can't seem to put a halt to these behaviors.

But there is a way. What it's going to take is the adoption of a whole new ethic. A new global principle, a species-wide agreement to apply a new and striking standard arising out of a new and striking understanding of what is true about ourselves and our Maker.

We're not a dumb species. We've put a man on the moon. We've cracked the code of the human genome. We've discovered cures for many diseases. We've created astonishing technologies. We can do this, too. But…as in days past when we've been challenged to consider new notions…(*"What? The Sun does not revolve around the Earth? Nonsense!"*…*"What? We need to sterilize our hands between surgical procedures? Nonsense!"*)…we're going to need some Idea Heroes now.

CRED

I'm going to assume that you're open to exploring a new approach to the matter of what role the essential energy of life can play in your experience, or you wouldn't have read this far. We've been discussing the first three steps of this approach in general terms. Here, now, are those ideas in a concise list:

1   Presume that a Higher Power exists.
2   Describe the Higher Power as an energy that can be physically felt.
3   Decide to call that feeling Pure Love.

Now let's explore a fourth step we haven't mentioned yet:

4   Make an important switch. Replace *thought* with *emotion* as the item in your spiritual/metaphysical toolbox to which you'll now pay the most attention, and of which you'll make the most use.

This could be the most powerful decision you've made in your life. That will be especially true if the emotion you most often encourage is not the first emotion that comes up for *you* in any given situation, but rather, *God's feeling*.

How can we possibly guess what that would be? We don't have to guess, we know. If we accept the premise that God exists, and if we proceed within the boundaries of our New Definition Approach, we will know that God's feeling is always Pure Love. Not sometimes. Not now and then. Not once in a while. But always.

Always, and *all ways*, that's how Divinity's Energy *feels*.

Feeling is the language of the Soul, which is God, individualized. Emotion is the language of the Mind, which is thought, physicalized. The two are entirely different vibrations.

Unless they're not. Unless you meld them into one.

CRSO

Hold it. Just a second. That was a pretty radical idea you heard just now. Don't let that slip past you. This expands our new method of personal growth and spiritual development, turning it into a two-part process.

The first half of that new method would be to switch out *thought* for *emotion* in your process of personal growth. The second half would be to meld *your emotion* with *God's feeling* in your process of spiritual development.

It's very clear to me that if we decide to define God's feeling as Pure Love, we suddenly (and to our enormous benefit) build a pathway for an immediate and wonderful involvement of God in our day-to-day lives.

The process of melding human emotion with divine feeling produces not only a place for Divinity's Energy to *show up* in our lives, but a way for it to actually be expressed and demonstrated. Experienced regularly, this will change not only each of us, but every person whose life we touch.

# 11.

Okay, I'm making some pretty bold statements here. I'm being this direct, this definitive, because I know that what's being explored here can be an answer to the God Dilemma.

By looking at God's feeling not through the lens of what some dogma or doctrine has told us, but through the window of the Soul (which is God in us), and then melding that feeling into our emotion, we are utilizing an enormously effective transformational tool. With it, we can expand an energy inwardly, and project an energy outwardly, that can change life for the better forever.

How? Why? Because (to repeat one more time for the sake of clarity and emphasis) God's feeling—that is, how Divine Energy is experienced—will always be most accurately described as Pure Love. When we meld the essence of our mentally-produced emotion and our spiritually-produced feeling, we raise the vibration of the overall energy with which our body is filled, and which we send into the world.

Now if people continue sticking with ancient messages or doctrines about how God feels, they may come up with energies of anger, judgment, or condemnation. The idea behind our New Definition Approach is that what the world would most benefit from right now is a civil rights movement for the Soul, freeing humanity at last from the oppression of its beliefs in a violent, angry, and vindictive God. This would open us to no longer expressing ourselves as a violent, angry, and vindictive species, given that *we would have a completely different role model to emulate.*

So, again, the invitation is to gently meld into your emotion, in every important choice-making moment, God's energy of Pure Love.

Now I need to make it clear that I am not suggesting for a minute that we should be denying or sublimating any emotion of our own. This is about *expanding* our emotion to include a feeling residing at the deepest place within us, which is where Divine Energy is located.

This is the founding energy, the originating vibration, the Essential Essence and the First Source. This is Who You Really Are, and all the rest is everything you've added to that: your Mind's thoughts, ideas, constructions, and stories.

None of these are even your *own*. They're a collection and conglomeration of what other people have told you, of what parents or guardians, families and tribes, religions and schools, books and sacred texts, movies and TV shows and yes, now even video games, have placed before you.

Very few of these sources have accurately reflected your True Identity. Our traditions have not said much about God In You, and the imageries and stories of our species have not exactly been centered around depicting Pure Love. So it would be unusual, to say the least, for anyone growing up in the prevailing culture on Earth to initially gravitate toward (much less be an early adopter of) these ideas.

On this planet we have not wanted to *teach* ourselves *about* ourselves in any ways which *contradict* ourselves. So we've remained stuck in our previous narratives. To say that God's energy would be felt as Pure Love for everything that's going on in your life would be a new narrative for sure.

Why in heaven's name (pun intended) would this be the energy that Divinity would project regarding the things have occurred in life that *you* have not loved?

It's because God understands that everything which occurs may be used—actually, is *intended* to be used—as a tool for your advancement in the process of your evolution.

Should *you* encounter life with this same understanding, each moment and event that you might not at first celebrate can be made remarkably easier to move through, because you are no longer resisting unhappy circumstances, but, instead, pouring Pure Love into them. This serves as a powerful shield, protecting you from negative energies that unwelcome events might otherwise have birthed within you.

CRED

I am far from being the first person to suggest using love *as a tool* in this way. Our species is currently blessed with wonderful teachers and authors offering programs and books recommending the use of love as a supportive and protective energy with which to confront difficult moments.

Byron Katie did so in her classic on this subject, *Loving What Is,* as well as her follow-up book, *A Thousand Names for Joy: Living in Harmony with the Way Things Are* (with her husband Stephen Mitchell). Marianne Williamson touched the heart of the matter in the remarkable global bestseller mentioned earlier, *A Return to Love.*

Other titles in this breed include *Whatever Arises, Love That,* and his follow up text, *Everything is Here to Help You,* from Matt Kahn. Also, *Sudden Awakening: Stop Your Mind, Open Your Heart, and Discover Your True Nature* by Eli Jaxon-Bear and Gangaji, *True Love: A Practice for Awakening the Heart* by Thich Nhat Hanh, and more.

These books, too, have no doubt been helpful to many. And what I'm going to say next is in no way meant as a criticism of their content, or a diminution of their value. It is but a humble suggestion that *all of us can go one step further.*

If we were to invite ourselves to experience the emotion that reflects what *God* feels as every event in life arises, we would seldom have to sit down and negotiate with each other to reach a collective agreement on when and how to react and proceed. We would *share a collectively held understanding*, which would *guide our choices and decisions.*

This new approach to life, jointly embraced, would cause the demonstration of Pure Love to occur *automatically,* in exactly the perfect way at exactly the perfect time. This is the power of an entire society holding an overarching idea collectively.

Let me offer you a small, if simplistic, example.

Everyone in your family is preparing to enjoy a delicious dessert of apple pie *à la Mode,* with just enough for a nice big piece for each person at the table. Then the doorbell rings. It's grandpa, paying a surprise visit. "Oh boy!" he exclaims, "Warm pie with ice cream! My favorite!" Nobody says, "But we've already cut one piece for each of us here." Of course not. Mom jumps up to bring another plate to the table. Dad pulls up an extra chair. Everyone else at the table races to slice their piece in half, even though it means they'll have a lot less. And you're the *first* to say, "Here, gramps! You're just in time!" You do this *automatically.* It's not a thought process, it's an emotional process. It's what you *feel like doing*, without even *thinking.* It's a group decision that's made without the need for consultation.

Again, this is an extremely simple example, used here for ease of illustration. But it is from the arising of just such emotion, on a larger scale, that the world can change overnight.

CRSO

So we see that it's not only about how we can *encounter* life's events, it's about how we can *create* them. It's about using not just the *protective* power, but the *productive* power, of the God that so many of us believe exists. *Finally*, we will have found a way to harness that energy, to focus it, and to project it intentionally.

When we expand how we use and experience Pure Love—enlarging its purpose from Protection to Production—we will have answered the question *What difference does it make?* regarding whether God exists or not.

This will require a fifth and final step in solving the God Dilemma:

5. Decide to *put into action* the specific feeling that God is defined as. Not just by creating and experiencing the emotion with which you respond to any given moment, but also by honing your ability to create *future* moments through the use of Pure Love as a tool of manifestation.

Substituting the highest and best emotion we can create for the thoughts that we habitually think could result in some very different decisions. Some really major choices. Some totally daring actions that could change both our personal lives, and the world that we touch.

I am engaging here, of course, in speculation. I could be wrong about all of this. But I believe that when we embrace the *feeling* that our newly defined God *is,* and allow it to flow freely in us, through us, and as us—and then *project it forward* into our tomorrows as a *creative force*—we are employing and magnifying, focusing and directing God's Essential Essence, and the world we touch lights up with love.

This is called enlightenment.

It is my idea that this occurs in any group or society, large or small, which decides that *everyone* is going to get a piece of the pie.

# 12.

*Should* everyone get a piece of the pie? Should all people share in the good life?

That's a question which humans have been attempting, through the various laws of their various societies, to answer forever.

Must the blessings of life be *earned?* Or is it reasonable in an Advanced Civilization to presume that everyone *in* that civilization will automatically share in the most beneficial offerings *of* that civilization?

If you'll forgive the repetition, a drop of clean, pollutant-free water once in a lifetime might be an example. The benefits of electricity in this, the first half of the 21$^{st}$ century, could be another. Indoor plumbing might be a third. Dare we even mention the hope that an Advanced Civilization would collectively devise a way to stop 650 of its children from dying of starvation every hour?

It's my suspicion that a collective idea that there are things which people should be *required* to do to receive life's blessings *on Earth* may very well be rooted in a collective idea that there are things which people are required to do to receive God's blessings *in Heaven*.

Could I be absolutely right about that? Is it possible that many people (perhaps *most* people, if eight out of ten say they believe in God) have engaged in the creation of a Rewards-Must-Be-Earned *culture* based on a Rewards-Must-Be-Earned *theology?*

What I am seeing is that these same people appear to believe that this earn-your-way model is a society's highest version of itself. Many have decided that Every Man for Himself is a far superior way to proceed than All For One and One For All—the motto of the title characters in *The Three Musketeers* by the nineteenth-century French author Alexandre Dumas. Dumas was either way ahead of his time, or hopelessly outmoded and lagging behind humanity's elevation as an Advanced Civilization. Which do you think?

But forget about the expectation of humans for just a moment. Must the love of *God* be earned? Is Divinity incapable of giving love to sentient beings simply because it is God's nature to do so, whether certain beings "deserve it" or not? Could the offering of love to someone who does *not* "deserve it" be the *height* of Pure Love?

CRSD

At some point we have to make a decision. What rings true in the deepest part of our being? Do we declare the truth to be what we have been *told* that it is, or what we intuitively *sense* that it is?

Oh, and there's another decision we have to make. This may be the biggest decision of all: Whose feeling shall we use to *determine* whether Pure Love is being expressed, the feeling of the person expressing it, or the feeling of the one affected by it?

Shouldn't the impact on another be positive—or at least not hurtful? If it feels positive for the first person, but hurtful for the second (as it probably would for a person in an electric chair), is it properly defined as Pure Love?

I think this is the kind of question that the American sociologist Milton J. Bennett must have been mulling over when he coined the term The Platinum Rule in the 1970s as a replacement for The Golden Rule.

Platinum is more valuable than gold, and Bennett wanted to come up with a statement that he considered might be more valuable as humans seek to understand what love for another is really about. His rule? "Do unto others as *they* would have it done unto *them*."

Do you see how this turns everything around? Now life's behavioral standard becomes not to treat others as *we* want to be treated, but to treat others as *they* want to be treated. This reinforces a spiritual experience that "we are all one" (hats off, Monsieur Dumas), in that it demonstrates that we want to feel, and are willing to feel, what others tell us *they* feel, not just what we feel.

Just a short time thinking about this will reveal that there could be differences—and the spiritual path of melding another's feelings *with my own* is an expression of Pure Love, if ever there was one.

This does not mean I must *agree* with another's feeling, but it does mean that my expression of love for another causes me to take their feelings into account, making those feelings as present within me as my own. This renders it far more possible for me to speak and act in a way that honors another's feelings, even if I do disagree with them.

So we are not talking here about allowing anyone to do anything they wish, simply because they "feel like it." You do not have to say "go ahead" to your 7-year-old grandson because he announces that he feels like jumping off the roof to see if he can fly. You do not have to allow someone to smoke in your non-smoking home because someone "feels like" doing so.

Let us be clear, then, that noticing feelings does not mean in every case complying with them. *Honoring* another's feelings creates harmony, even if disagreement creates contrast. Contrast does not have to produce conflict, difference does not have to produce division, and variance does not have to produce violence in our lives.

Here's a question to consider: Is it true that the way in which a person is *affected* by someone's expression of love is a fair and accurate measure of whether it is God's Pure Love that's being expressed? Should the effect on another have anything to do with it? I want to suggest that it should be the *ultimate* measure, if we're going to call what we are doing "love for the other."

But now, to be fair, it must be acknowledged that both the question and the answer here are being considered within the context that neither of the people involved are facing mental health challenges, which could impair their ability to send or receive Pure Love.

We know, of course, that God is not facing such challenges, so here is a daring theological thought: God's Pure Love is never expressed in a way that has *as its intention* the hurting or damaging or punishing of anyone.

Before you reject that idea outright (if you were tempted to do so), let's all be Idea Heroes and just explore this question once more for good measure: Shouldn't the impact on another of one's expression of love be positive? If it feels positive on the sending end, but negative on the receiving end, is it properly defined as Pure Love?

This is not an idle inquiry. This is a necessary question for members of any caring society to ask, and it rises to the level of a critical inquiry when matters of quality of life—to say nothing of life and death—are involved.

Is revenge an expression of Pure Love? Is self-righteousness? Is obedience under duress?

Wait. Maybe an even more comprehensive solution to the God Dilemma invites a more precise and sharply defined description of the feeling that we're calling Pure Love.

I did my best in Chapter 8 to offer that, but it took 177 words over two long paragraphs for me to do it. Let me further clarify that now, but with a much shorter version.

"Pure Love is that energy which, when expressed, creates happiness in the sender and is sent with the intention of creating what the receiver also feels as happiness, allowing the receiver to respond freely and genuinely without losing the love being sent."

In even fewer words: Pure Love is unconditional.

What do you think? Do you agree? Maybe read it again. Take it in and roll it around.

Do you agree?

CRSO

Now, it could be fairly argued that the one who is expressing love cannot be responsible for how their energy is received. A particular receiver could be at first uneasy with it or have a need to actually reject it for some inner reason unknown to the sender. All of this is true.

Yet if the love that is expressed is Pure Love, the sender would want, expect, hope for, ask for, and need nothing in return. And that kind of freedom, experienced by the receiver of the love, to respond in a way that is totally genuine, would very likely not produce a feeling of being injured.

If we all agreed with the definition of Pure Love offered just above, the very big decisions, really major choices, and totally daring actions we spoke of earlier actually *could* result.

I'm going to say that the New Definition Approach to understanding God may not only solve a *theological* dilemma, but may also be the best chance we have of solving our human dilemma of how to create, at last, the life on this planet of which we have so long dreamed.

# 13.

Is it conceivable that a single new idea in humanity's hundreds of collectively held concepts about a Higher Power could cause us to change our attitudes and behaviors so dramatically that our species would at last be freed of the anger and violence which our old behaviors produced?

Yes.

Can the New Definition Approach—simply defining God as self-conscious, self-aware energy eternally projecting a feeling called Pure Love—mend the tear in the fabric of our global society?

Yes.

My answers are yes. But even if we only thought *hypothetically* that such a thing is possible, would it be worth giving it a try?

My mind tells me that it all depends on how much emotional and cultural upheaval would be caused by adopting this "single new idea."

In assessing that, I wonder if revising our definition of God would be really so upsetting. How do the eight out of ten people who declare their belief in a Higher Power *currently* define this Divine Entity? Is our collective culture deeply attached to a particular notion?

Nope. As already noted, it's all over the map on this. Given this ambiguity and lack of species-wide commitment to a singular and particular definition, would it be so utterly unacceptable for people to broadly agree that God is, plain and simple, an intelligent, self-conscious, self-aware essential essence and magnificently expressive energy that we could call Pure Love?

Does this seem like a notion so at variance with humanity's dominant concept of a benevolent Higher Power as to be immediately rejected by the majority of God-believers?

Or is it possible that the *opposite* might be true; that the idea might seem so logically and theologically on the mark that we would wonder *what took us so long* to get there, and that it would be agreed to and welcomed by the largest number of God-believers instantly?

What do you think? Do you feel that this new definition of God could be transformative enough for humanity to actually impact life on Earth in a positive way?

Ah, that's where you come in.

CR&O

Can you imagine sending a letter or an email containing loving thoughts to a political leader whose actions, decisions, and speeches you abhor?

Can you imagine reaching out with love to a neighbor who has slandered you and caused you to lose your friends, or a fellow worker who has lied and caused you to lose your job?

Can you imagine greeting with love someone who has gained the affection of, and then lured from you, your life partner?

If you can, you understand what Pure Love is about. If you can, you remember the words that were shared with us not very recently, but that are perhaps more relevant at this moment in our history than ever before.

"Love your enemies, bless them that curse you, do good to them that hate you, and pray for them which despitefully use you, and persecute you."

So spoke Jesus.

You may also remember this, from another source: "Monks, even if bandits were to savagely sever you, limb by limb, with a double-handled saw, even then, whoever of you harbors ill will at heart would not be upholding my teaching.

"Monks, even in such a situation you should train yourselves thus: Neither shall our minds be affected by this, nor for this matter shall we give vent to evil words, but we shall remain full of concern and pity, with a mind of love, and we shall not give in to hatred.

"On the contrary, we shall live projecting thoughts of universal love to those very persons, making them, as well as the whole world, the object of our thoughts of universal love—thoughts that have grown great, exalted and measure-less."

So spoke the Buddha.

The question now before the house: Is the behavior suggested by these ideas within reach of the average person?

☙❧

Now you might be tempted to say, No. *You're quoting the world's greatest saints and sages, and expecting regular, normal people to live up to that.*

Yet on this turns the whole New Definition Approach to understanding God and solving the God Dilemma. That solution is *based* on the very premise that embracing and expressing

Pure Love—even for those who have hurt us or are our ene-mies—is possible for the average person.

And the fact that it *was* taught by all those spiritual messen-gers through all the ages is *evidence* that the behavior *must* be attainable by the average person.

Would our most revered teachers have given us instructions that they knew were impossible for people to follow? Why would they have done that? Was it their intention to frustrate humankind forever, or to heal humankind forever? Which do you think?

Unless we're willing to label Jesus, the Buddha, and every other spiritual teacher through the ages as scam artists and char-latans, we have to assume that it was their deep-seated clarity that their teachings absolutely can be applied in real, everyday life by real, everyday people.

And they can be.

You and I can do this.

We don't have to be saints, either. We don't have to be uncommonly virtuous. We simply have to *want* to live in a certain way. We can't just *wish* that we could, or *hope* that we could, or *wonder* if we could. We have to *know* that we could, if we simply made the firm decision to do so.

This much, though, is true: We won't achieve this change of behavior overnight, nor will it be achieved with half-hearted effort. People have been trying for centuries to live up to the words of our greatest spiritual teachers, and we have not found it easy. Yet this way of moving through the world does not have to be burdensome—nor *will* it be if it arises out of true and deep desire.

So, what could make it your true and deep desire?

I'm proposing that it would be the remembrance of how utterly *complete* you felt inside every time you've offered your love to someone who by all rights didn't "deserve" it, and whose words or actions may have actually, by every normal standard, warranted your anger.

Have you ever demonstrated that kind of love in your life? Of course, you have.

I'm going to invite you to think of that time now.

Think of a person who hurt you, and to whom you showed love afterward. (Really do this little exercise, as a favor to yourself.) Remember a time when you acted lovingly toward someone who did not "deserve" your love, and really had no right to expect it.

Did you do this at a family reunion? During a holiday gathering? In a personal, private conversation? Wherever it was, remember when that moment ended. Just close your eyes for a second and put yourself back into how you felt as you drove home…or when they drove away.

Leave your reading here, close your eyes and let yourself remember this now.

CRSO

Nice work. Good job.

Now, can you put that feeling into one word?

Give it a try. Maybe even write that word right here in this book, in the space below. Put into one word how you felt

CRSO

Do you see? *You have already done this.* This is not even a question of trying out a new behavior. This is a matter of simply repeating what you have done before.

I'm going to suggest to you that in the moment when you showed love to that particular other person, you completely altered any idea you ever had about yourself as being small. You also changed your idea about what was most important to you. In that moment you decided that what was most important to you regarding others is not who *they* are, but who *you* are.

I promise you that once you become used to experiencing who you are at that level, you will not want to return to any other way of being. You will know yourself as whole and uninjured—and, in a very real sense, *unable* to be injured.

Now here's an idea that may make loving your enemies easier. As you deeply consider this concept of stepping into your wholeness by doing so, choose to embrace and appreciate the deep relationship between the words "wholeness" and "holiness."

Know that the way of being described here is not only about being "wholly human," but about being a "holy" human. Try to not flinch from that description. Being holy does not require you to be "saintly" or "unworldly" or "unnaturally virtuous." In fact, just the opposite. It invites you to be who you *naturally are.*

The sense of yourself that you experienced when you openly loved someone who angered or hurt you is *who you really are.* You knew it the moment you felt it. You felt wholly you, and holy you—*and you had a sense that the two are one.* It's what my wife calls a "glimpse" of the larger reality of you.

And don't worry about others imagining that you're suddenly seeing yourself as "holier than thou." Your words and actions will show that you know that *everyone* is holy. You demonstrate this when you love others even as they are not reflecting their *own* wholeness. It is especially in such moments that your showing them love gives them back to themselves.

You are demonstrating that you recognize that we are all holy when you are in touch with and are expressing God's energy of Pure Love. This is not an energy that you call *for* when you feel you need it, but that you call *forth*. You bring it forward from within you, as opposed to asking for it from outside of you. This is exactly what you did in that moment when you showed love to one who did not "deserve" your love.

With your actions, you revealed that they *did* "deserve" your love; that their worthiness was not based on what they were doing or have done, but who they are at the core of their being and have always been.

By your choice you have shown that you recognize—that is, know again, or re-*cognize*—their holiness.

We see then that all of us are holy, not because of how we are acting, but because of who we are at the level of essence: a part of God. If you feel that God is holy, then you will clearly see that you, too, are holy. Because the one thing that God is *not* is holier than thou. How can God be holier that Itself? It cannot.

Now if you think that you are not *part* of God, we have a different story. But, of course, you are. The Essential Essence that is Life Itself is expressed throughout the Universe—and that includes, of course, you.

God has been using life to convince you of that from the very beginning. Will you allow yourself now to be assured?

I would like to offer here a passage from the book *Conversations with God,* which I have never forgotten. Type it up, print it out, and tape it to your bathroom mirror:

"You are goodness and mercy and compassion and understanding. You are peace and joy and light. You are forgiveness and patience, strength and courage, a helper in time of need, a comforter in time of sorrow, a healer in time of injury, a teacher in times of confusion. You are the deepest wisdom and the highest truth; the greatest peace and the grandest love. You *are* these things. And in moments of your life you have *known* yourself *as* these things.

"*Choose now to know yourself as these things always.*"

# 14

Perhaps all of us could be convinced that we humans are holy—
and that this whole idea that Pure Love is who we really are
might be actually *workable*—if we could see it demonstrated in
even the most extreme situations.

Can you imagine, for instance, blessing someone who tried
to kill you, and nearly succeeded?

A Polish man named Karol Józef Wojtyła not only imagined
it, he did it. He went to the jail cell of Mehmet Ali Ağca, who
shot him six times at close range on May 13, 1981, and gave the
man his blessing after a long talk together. Mr. Wojtyła was better
known at the time as Pope John Paul II, but that title made him
no less human, no less one of us. But he was a person who had
made a firm decision about how he wanted to *be* in his life.

The Pope and his attempted assassin became pen pals during
the time the latter was serving his life sentence, exchanging
letters frequently. And in 2000, the Pontiff asked the civil
authorities in Italy to pardon and release Mehmet Ali Ağca.
That request was granted.

So we see that when it comes to showing love to those who
have acted unkindly is something you have done, something a
Pope has done, and, I'm sure, something that a great many other

people have done. One simply has to make a decision: *Pure Love is who I am; Pure Love is what I choose to express.*

CRSO

Now does any of this mean, in a society based on New Definitions of God and Pure Love, that if one person deliberately kills another, the assassin should, after serving jail time, ultimately be pardoned and freed? Or should our response to people who have committed murder be to murder them?

Is there a place between these alternatives that would and could demonstrate Pure Love?

If you created your own religion, an idea raised in Chapter 5, what would it look like in the "real world"? If our entire civilization lived by your ideas, how would we act, what would we do?

Let's consider examples not quite as dramatic as blessing a man who tried to kill you. Let's look at some things that occur in everyday life.

If everyone was practicing your religion, would merchants and corporations, for instance, charge "whatever the traffic will bear" for their products and services, or would they deliberately set a price that generates less profit, but helps more people have a better life?

(In the first quarter of the 21st century some businesses were known to mark up their products or services 200%, 50%, or even 10,000%, depending on the total cost of what they offered and its "salability" in the marketplace.)

Would people be required by local custom or convention, for instance, to submit to practices with which they may profoundly disagree, such as female genital mutilation—also referred to as female genital cutting?

(In 2020, the practice was common in 30 countries in western, eastern, and north-eastern Africa, in parts of the Middle East and Asia, and within some immigrant communities in Europe, North America and Australia. As of April 2020, 38 *U.S. states* had passed specific laws that prohibit FGM, with the remaining 12 states having no laws banning the procedure whatsoever.)

Would individuals who have divorced and wish to marry another be allowed to have their wedding take place in a space where their religion is celebrated if their previous spouse still lives, and the previous marriage has not been annulled?

(As of May 2020, Catholics in that circumstance were not permitted to marry in the church. Nor could they, for that matter, receive communion at Mass.)

Would couples of the same sex be accorded, everywhere in the world, the legal and social benefits of marriage?

(As of October 2019, just 30 of the 195 countries in the world had legalized same sex marriage.)

What, if anything at all, would you predict would shift in our individual and group behaviors if we all gravitated toward *your* religion?

I'm going to guess that plenty would change if your religion shifted the present viewpoint of every theology on the planet. For example, where would our theologies be if we taught of a God who stood by this promise found in the Bible: "Judge not, and ye shall not be judged. Condemn not, and ye shall not be condemned."? (Luke 6:37)

CRSO

Are we ready to accept the reality of a Deity who has no need, no desire, and no intention to judge and condemn, so long as we do not judge or condemn others?

Does the Biblical passage mean that a Jew who does not judge or condemn others, or a Muslim who does not judge or condemn others, or a Bahá'í who does not judge or condemn others, or an *atheist* who does not judge or condemn others, will not be judged or condemned by God?

No, we are told by some religions, that is not what it means. God will not only judge and condemn those who belong to the "wrong" religion or no religion at all, God will punish them with eternal and unrelenting torture.

Of course, the contradiction between the Biblical promise and some of those teachings is obvious. So, did Luke not understand what he was told—or is it *we* who have *gotten it wrong ever since?*

The biggest part of humanity's God Dilemma is that every theology on the planet is founded on the idea of a befuddled Higher Power who is the creator of all and the source of everything yet can somehow be displeased with something that the Higher Power itself has empowered.

Displeased *enough* (to put a fine point on it) to send a soul to hell for particular "offenses" that many might feel to be (dare it be said) trivial. Or certainly not grounds for Eternal Damnation.

May I give you one example? I've used this before, in previous writings, and I'm not making this up. And please hear me when I say that I have many beautiful memories of my formative spiritual experience as a member of the Catholic Church. It brought me a belief in God, and in what I now want to call higher realities—such as everlasting life. That said, the Church teaches that missing Sunday Mass without a justifiable reason (having to work, needing to care for an elderly parent or a sick child, etc.) is punishable by everlasting torture in the fires of hell, unless the sin is revealed in a confessional and forgiven by a priest before the offender dies.

I remember being scared out of my mind about this as a child. I grew up in a Catholic family, but I have to be truthful and say that I didn't go to Mass every single Sunday. Most Sundays, yes. But did I play hooky once in a while—especially during the summer—and head to the playground for a little baseball? Yep. Like a "bad" 12-year-old, I did that, telling my Dad I wanted to sleep in and would be going to 11 o'clock Mass (he always went to 9 o'clock Mass and usually took me with him).

But one particular Sunday I was cured forever of offending God in this way. I was almost hit by a car on my walk home from the ballgame, having crossed a street a little carelessly. My heart was almost pounding out of my chest that night. Not so much because of my near miss with a big silver Buick but thinking about hell and how I would have gone straight there and suffered eternal damnation had I died on that corner.

That sent me rushing to Confession the next day, I can promise you.

Today, as an adult, I must ask: what if a person who misses Mass does not judge or condemn others for missing Mass? And what if that person judges and condemns no one else for *anything*? Will that person also then neither be judged nor condemned, as Luke told us Jesus promised?

A close look at all of this reveals that our species has for millennia wanted to have its cake and eat it, too. We've wanted a Deity who tells *us* to judge not and neither condemn, but then adds: "Do as I say, don't do as I do. I *have* to judge and condemn. I'm God."

This may be uncomfortable to some as we look at all this more closely, but taken together, there is a whole list of things that human religions teach is displeasing to the Higher Power. Divorce (already mentioned), swearing, giving alms in front of another, laying up treasure on Earth, looking lustfully at someone who is not your marriage partner, worrying about the future, being proud, dancing, listening to certain music…

These are not (so far as we know) damnable offenses, but they don't exactly put us in the best standing with God. It has not been made clear what displeasing God results in, but it can't be good. Especially since God never forgives anyone for anything.

# 15

That was not meant as a joke. That was not a bit of satire. That was meant to be taken literally. God never forgives anyone for anything. If you were counting on God's forgiveness, it's time that you were told the truth. You're not going to receive it. Ever.

I can now imagine some readers thinking: *Wait a minute! I thought you said that God was Pure Love. Now you're telling me that God won't forgive us for our transgressions?* 🖋

That's right. That's exactly what I'm telling you.

Let's go back to the dining room table with Grampa and the apple pie to help us understand this.

Just as the grandson is saying, excitedly, "Here Grampa, you're just in time!" and happily reaching out to hand him half of his desert, his 4-year-old sister says, "No! I wanna give Grampa *my* pie. I was *first!*" She pushes her pie ahead of her brother's, and in the process knocks over her glass of milk. Now there's milk all over the table, and a ton of it is dripping into Grampa's lap. What does he do? He jumps up and shouts at the little girl, "What's the *matter* with you! You should know better! Go to your room, and don't come out for the rest of the summer! I'll teach *you* to spill milk in my lap!"—right?

Of course not. He just looks at her and says, "I forgive you."—right?

Of course not. Grampa knows that forgiveness is not even part of the equation. He neither punishes the little girl, nor does he forgive her. He actually *comforts* her. As she cries about what she did, he says, "Oh, sweetheart, it's okay," and moves over to give her a big hug. "I love you," he says.

Yes, it's another simplistic example, but again I offer it to make a point. Forgiveness is not part of this equation for a very good reason. Grampa understands that a 4-year-old is going to make childish mistakes.

Now, many people like to think of humans as highly evolved (in spite of the fact that we're acting like 4-year-olds), but in truth, humanity has just emerged from its infancy on this planet. In their book *New World New Mind*, Robert Ornstein and Paul Ehrlich placed this in perspective with one mind-boggling paragraph, which I have quoted in books and lectures frequently, because I consider it to be a master stroke of clarity on this subject. They wrote:

"Suppose Earth's history were charted on a single year's calendar, with midnight January 1 representing the origin of the Earth and midnight December 31 the present. Then each day of Earth's "year" would represent 12 million years of actual history. On that scale, the first form of life, a simple bacterium, would arise sometime in February. More complex life-forms, however, come much later; the first fishes appear around November 20. The dinosaurs arrive around December 10 and disappear on Christmas Day. The first of our ancestors recognizable as human would not show up until the afternoon of December 31. Homo sapiens—our species—would emerge at around 11:45 pm…and all that has happened in recorded history would occur in the final minute of the year."

This tells us all we need to know about how much progress has been made in the evolution of our species. We see, then, that God has neither need nor cause to forgive us, any more than we have a need to "forgive" a 4 year-old for something that little children do. In this context we see that "Vengeance is mine, sayeth the Lord" may be the biggest spiritual misunderstanding of all time.

Should humanity reach the point where it embraces the idea that the Essential Essence we call God is a fully conscious and totally self-aware *energy* that can be *felt*—and should we agree that this feeling is what we call Pure Love—the explanation about forgiveness being offered here will never be necessary again. In the present moment, however, it's important to put the clarification into this text, for without it, we may find it more difficult to collectively create a solution to the God Dilemma.

CR&O

I have addressed the topic of forgiveness before, in previous writings, but I'm not going to be even a little bit shy about reiterating what I've shared earlier, as I believe that new ideas about God should receive repeated and unsparing review.

Anyone who would even consider revolutionary proposals regarding our Deity should be offered more than a one-time passing glance at them. Unrelenting examination and merciless evaluation of their principle points must be invited, in a tenacious and unflinching search for any defect in logic or flaw in conclusions.

So I am saying again here, as I have written before (using some of these exact words), that God does not forgive anyone for anything. The proposition is that forgiveness is unnecessary, having been replaced in the process of Divine Balance with a more searingly powerful form of Pure Love: understanding.

First, Divinity understands Who and What It Is, and so It is aware that It cannot be hurt or injured, damaged or diminished, wronged or offended in any way. This means that Divinity would never be disappointed in us or frustrated with us, annoyed with us or angry with us, nor would It seek or need to be vengeful—not even in the name of celestial "justice," as some religions suggest.

Secondly, Divinity understands Who and What humans are, and so It is aware that *we do not* understand who and what *we* are, and so do and say things that could be expected of little children—which only a tyrannical parent would need to forgive, much less punish.

Now let me add something to this, to place "forgiveness" into context. Forgiveness *can* be a helpful tool in the earliest stages of one's spiritual development, as it can assist beginning spiritual students in their initial attempts to overcome anger or release their resentments. Yet the time comes in everyone's spiritual maturing when forgiveness is not only no longer useful but can actually be an obstacle to continued spiritual growth.

If training wheels on a child's bicycle are never discarded, the child will never learn the secret of balance. As spiritual children, we are finding the balance point between our humanity and our divinity. This is the time when we can set aside the tool of forgiveness, realizing that it was useful to help us find our humanity, but that it is not needed in order to express our divinity. Indeed, the fullest expression of divinity precludes it.

The balance point, then, is this: use forgiveness as an elementary device if it helps you and another feel better but see if *not* making another feel they've done something requiring your forgiveness might be even more healing to you both. This is not done by completely ignoring what has happened, but rather, by understanding how it could have happened in the first place. This is a far more advanced tool, and a far more effective way of moving forward.

# 16

In the mind of the master, understanding is engaged at two levels. At level one, masters understand who they really are. They are aware of their true identity as Individuations of Divinity. At level two, masters understand how someone could have done what has been done. Perhaps they, themselves, have done such a thing at one point in their own evolutionary journey to mastery. Maybe not on the same scale, but with the same energetic content.

All of us have said or done things which we felt, in the moment, were justified—or at least understandable. In fact, no one does anything inappropriate, given their model of the world. A 4-year-old's model of the world is clearly not the same as a 40-year-old's model, and a 40-year-old's is obviously not the same as an 80-year-old's model.

Looking back on our lives, most of us can see clearly what made us say and do what we said and did when we said and did it. That doesn't make all of it commendable, but it can make all of it understandable.

Seen from this perspective, our forgiveness of the self or another has no advanced spiritual function, in that it would only have meaning in the case of a spiritual entity (an individual soul, or God) having been spiritually injured. And such a thing is impossible.

Again, this does not mean that we condone everything that has been done, nor that we approve of certain things being done again, but it does mean that we understand how and why something could have occurred. And understanding replaces forgiveness in the mind of the master.

That is a spiritually revolutionary principle, and you are being invited to remember this axiom always: *Understanding replaces forgiveness in the mind of the master.*

From a spiritual standpoint, the idea that you need to forgive someone else for something they have done *denies the reality of who you are* as an Individuation of Divinity, and suggests that the Essential Essence that is you can somehow be hurt or damaged by the actions of another.

From that spiritual standpoint you know that your body can be affected, and your mind can be impacted, but your soul cannot be touched in any negative way. Even your life itself cannot and will not end, for as an eternal being you will live forever and ever, and even forevermore.

As you take into account these truths, it will become apparent to you that a person who has done something "bad" with regard to you is demonstrating by their actions that they have forgotten who they really are. They must be living in a reality in which they feel that they, themselves, have been injured in some way by life, and need to respond to that injury.

Knowing this allows the serious student of spiritual mastery to ask a profound and often healing question of people who have attempted to injure us: "What hurts you so bad that you feel you have to hurt me in order to heal it?"

You can ask the same question of yourself if another says they feel injured by something that you have said or done.

"What hurts me so bad that I felt I had to hurt someone else in order to heal it?" The self-understanding that this can promote could be far more useful and more deeply beneficial than self-forgiveness.

Self-forgiveness often opens the door for people to do the same kind of thing over and over again. You may have actually examined yourself about this kind of thing, thinking something like, "I don't know why I keep doing that. It never works, and I don't even like the part of me that talks like that." But when self-*understanding* replaces self-forgiveness, true healing can begin. Therefore, seek at first to heal the hurt within, so that the chance of hurting others again with the same outward behavior drops to near zero.

Then know that, from a purely spiritual perspective, the idea that you need to forgive yourself for something you have done with regard to another denies the reality of their sovereignty, rejecting the truth of who they really are, based on your thought that another aspect of God can be offended, damaged, or hurt by you. Their body can be affected, and their mind can be impacted, but their soul cannot be touched in any negative way.

Now to be absolutely clear, a person who is sufficiently advanced in their thinking to comprehend and embrace, on a theological level, what has just been said here will reject the idea that this gives them carte blanche to treat others in any way which the other would consider cruel or heartless. Nor is it about being cavalier or indifferent to the experience of others.

No one who is seeking to move to a level of spiritual mastery would adopt such a posture—and no one who is reading this book is encouraged to do so—*but just the opposite.*

# 17.

Do you have the patience to go more deeply into this? I hope so, because there is another reason why God has no need to forgive humans for anything they have done—and this may be the most important reason of all.

God has no need to forgive humans for anything they have done because God is clear that every act is an act of love.

This is true categorically and without exception. It applies now and throughout human history. One cannot point to a single act, choice, or decision that did not arise out of love. Even the most heinous crime, the most horrible offense or misdeed, is or was an expression of love for something. When one thinks about it deeply, it becomes clear that this is true.

*What, then, of fear? What of anger? What of hatred? What of evil? What of violence and killing? Surely, these can't be expressions of Love,* one might protest. But they are. If you didn't love something, you wouldn't fear anything. If you didn't love something, you couldn't hate something else. If you didn't love something desperately, you couldn't even begin to think of using desperate measures, including violence or even killing, as a means of getting it, keeping it, or protecting it.

If you didn't love something intensely, you could never be

angry about either never having it, or having it taken from you.

Thieves act out of love. They love something so much that they desperately want to have it, and because they know of no other way they can easily get it, they steal it. The same is true of people who commit other crimes. Even the most horrific crimes. Rape. Murder. Child abuse. All are acts arising out of someone's love of something—even if their idea of what love *is,* is a deeply distorted understanding.

A person who has come to fully comprehend this would, then, respond to any act of another that many would judge to be despicable by asking a slightly altered version of our earlier inquiry: "What have you loved so much that you found yourself doing what you have done?"

(Could this have been a question that a Pope asked his assailant?)

When we search for the answer to this question we see clearly, if sadly, that their acts were acts of love. Undisputedly contorted acts, for sure. Not condoned or approved of by our society, and not justified or defended by these explanations. But understood. And thus, held in a different way by God. (As demonstrated by a Pope.)

Divinity understands that the problem is not that human beings do not love, but that many human beings do not know *how* to love in every instance in ways that would be welcomed by *them* if they were receiving love from another in the same form.

God sees us as we are: little children, without the emotional or spiritual maturity to truly understand the impact or the consequences of our actions. We have not learned how to do unto others as they would have it done unto them, to quote that Platinum Rule created by Milton Bennett.

And there is a minuscule percentage of humans who do things that are ugly beyond measure and that, from our commonly held point of view, seem totally unforgivable. Indeed, it would take a person who is deeply in touch with Who They Are and Who They Choose to Be to forgive some of the things that some people have done (as per the example of Pope John Paul II).

On a theological level it would take — dare we think it? — a God who is so loving that forgiveness is not deemed necessary, replaced by the absolution of total understanding

The message here is that, difficult as it may be for us to embrace, all things emerge from a single energy in the universe, which in our language we call love.

Why do 4-year-old children play with matches while hiding in the closet, knowing that they shouldn't be doing this? Perhaps *especially* knowing they shouldn't be doing it? Is it the love of mischief? Of discovery? Of adventure?

Do we make the child pay for their mistake for the rest of their life, even if they started a fire that burned the house down? Or do we comfort the child in the time of their distress over what they have done, and continue to soothe that person throughout their life in moments when they still can't let go of guilt as they remember the calamity they caused?

I want to tell you a story.

I never played with matches and burned the house down, but I did break my mother's most treasured family heirloom. It was a delicate vase that was kept on the mantlepiece above the fireplace. My mother had gotten it from her mother, who had gotten it from her mother, who had gotten it from her mother. One of those things. An item that can't be replaced.

Of course, my Mom had asked me a hundred times, "Please, sweetheart, don't touch the vase," whenever she saw me getting anywhere near it. And naturally, I had to do it. I couldn't stop myself. I had to know what made it so special that it was not even allowed to be touched. So, one day when my mother wasn't looking, I pulled a stool over to the fireplace, used it to get me high enough to look closely at the vase, and stared at it for what I'm sure was a full minute. But just looking wasn't good enough for me. I had to—just *had* to—reach up and touch it.

I was what—eight, nine? It doesn't matter. I knew right from wrong. I knew what my Mom had asked me not to do. There was not a single doubt in my mind that I was doing something I ought not to have been doing. I don't know what got into me. Was it something as simple and childish as the love of doing the Totally Forbidden? I don't know, but of course you know how the story ended. I knocked over the vase and it crashed to the floor.

You also must know that my heart sank lower than a heart could go. I knew that my mother's heart would be broken into more pieces than the vase. And it was. I could see it on her face as she rushed into the room from the kitchen, where she'd heard the crash.

I will never forget that moment as long as I live. My mother looked at me, looked at the vase, looked back at me, saw my devastation, my hopeless dismay, and made a choice right then and there.

Bringing herself to my level, she grasped me in her arms, pulled me as close as close could be, then held me apart again so that she could look squarely into my eyes. "Sweetheart," she said softly, almost in a whisper, "that is a vase…and you are my son. I love you more than any object in the world. Now go. Go outside and play." Then she squeezed me one more time and blessed my cheek with the sweetest kiss I ever received.

My mother understood how I could have done such a thing. She didn't need to have anything explained to her, and she didn't need to reach for clarity about what was most important to her.

I'd like to think that God is at least as nice as my mother. I know that in my life, I've created broken glass along the way, but I have an idea that when the whole game is over, I will be held in the arms of The Divine, and be blessed with the second sweetest kiss I ever received.

CRED

I know now that all actions—even utterly misguided ones—are understandable. The only reason we would call anything "unforgivable" is that we don't understand how anyone could do such a thing. But God does. And when we meld *our emotion* with *God's feeling*, we will, too.

Seeing ourselves with this increasing awareness, we will accept the invitation from life to create, as a solution to the God Dilemma, a new personal ethic, a new personal expression, a new personal experience. We will choose to stand as an exemplar, a living and continuing presentation, of the highest truth of life: Pure Love is what God is, and Pure Love is who we are.

# 18.

I made the statement early in this book that *what* we believe about God, the Higher Power, or life's Originating Energy impacts and determines, in a major way, how we create our life and life all around us. I said then that 80% of civil law in most of the countries of Europe and the West are based on Canon Law.

Since then I've been hoping to make the point that stepping away from what we have understood in the past to be "God's Word" and embracing now what our heart experiences as Pure Love is a wonderful way to inspire human society to adopt a new global ethic. Such a raising of our collective standards could finally help us put an end not only to our hugely damaging interactions, such as aggression and war, but to our very unkind communal norms and intolerant societal behaviors that also issue from ecclesiastical mandates.

It is those mandates which, from 1849 to 1978, prohibited Black men from being ordained as priests in the Church of Jesus Christ of Latter-day Saints. The church's justification was what was called "the Curse of Ham," preceded by the "Curse of Cain."

God is said to have punished Cain for killing his brother Abel by beating Cain about the face until his skin turned black.

Ham is said to have married a Black woman who, in turn, was said to have been a descendent of Cain…and Ham's son, Canaan, was cursed to a life of slavery by Ham's father, Noah, according to this ongoing Biblical saga.

Hence, a centuries-long declaration had been made—*in the Bible*, according to many ministers who preached it and congregants who accepted it—that dark-skinned people should be relegated to slavery.

I'm not making this up. Stories about both the "Curse of Cain" and the "Curse of Ham" are found in the book of Genesis, and both are too far-fetched to go into further here—but not far-fetched enough to stop a worldwide church from baldly declaring for 130 years that Black men were unworthy of the priesthood.

But it went beyond this one denomination. The "Curse of Cain" was also used to support a ban on ordaining Black men to most Protestant clergies until the 1960s in both the United States and Europe, an article in Wikipedia tells us.

The same article relates that "certain Catholic dioceses in the Southern United States adopted a policy of not ordaining Black men to oversee, administer the sacraments to, or accept confessions from White parishioners. This policy was not based on a 'curse of Cain' teaching but was justified by the widely held perception that slaves should not rule over their masters."

This notion, too, was used for decades to justify slavery in the American south, with Christian ministers routinely citing Biblical passages relating to, and purportedly supporting, slavery as an acceptable aspect of life.

The same kind of ecclesiastical authority was used, also, until the last quarter of the 20th century, to bar women from the priesthood in the Episcopal Church—a ban which was finally lifted in 1974. The *New York Times* pointed out in a story on July

19, 1997, that nearly 25 years later women were still barred from serving in 4 of the church's 113 dioceses, because the bishops there believed Christian tradition restricts the priesthood to men.

"And," the newspaper's story added, "the lack of uniformity reflects how unsettled the issue of women's ordination remains within the context of organized religion. Three of Judaism's four movements -- the Reform, the Conservative and the Reconstructionist -- ordain women as rabbis, but Orthodox Judaism does not."

(It still did not in 2020. Nor can women be ordained as priests in the Mormon church. Black Mormons finally, yes, but women, no.)

"In the Roman Catholic Church, Pope John Paul II has declared the issue closed," concluded the story, "arguing that Jesus established the precedent for a male priesthood by calling only men as his apostles."

So again, we see that there is that ever-present challenge of the God Dilemma faced by those who believe in a Higher Power: the lack of uniformity.

CRLEOD

But what about contemporary secular culture? Have any age-old "non-uniform" religious beliefs about people of color and women and other minorities seeped into today's society outside of church?

What do you think?

A March 2019 article by Julie Sprankles at SheKnows.com offers this:

"Watching a ball game, maybe even while enjoying a beer, is a pastime we tend to take for granted here in the U.S. But in October 2018, Iran made global headlines for a milestone moment—for the first time in 35 years, women were allowed to attend a sporting event (a soccer match between Iran and Bolivia). After the match, however, the country returned to its previous ban on such behavior that has been in place since the 1979 Islamic Revolution.

"The country's general prosecutor, Mohammad Jafar Montazeri, went so far as to proclaim he would order Tehran's government to legally prosecute any stadium officials who bend the rules for women."

The article went on to note that "certain countries, like Yemen and Saudi Arabia, operate on a 'male guardianship' system. Because this system essentially implies women are not full citizens, they must consult a spouse, brother, husband or son before making critical decisions about their own lives. This means no applying for a passport, no traveling abroad, and sometimes no leaving the house."

In the United States women could leave the house, but they could not vote until 1919. And they still had no formal workplace rights for 45 more years. The passage of Title VII of the Civil Rights Act of 1964 finally—*finally*—fixed that.

It is not news that people of color and of non-heterosexual orientation have likewise had to fight—and are still fighting—for basic human rights.

I'm not getting into all this here simply to present a shopping list of society's transgressions. I hope to make the point, *indelibly*, that there are real world consequences to what people have been thinking about God and have declared to be God's Word through the years.

The website of the Georgetown Law library notes that "discrimination continues to exist against minorities of all kinds, including towards members of the LGBTQ+ community.

Historically, anyone who strayed from the traditional gender roles assigned at birth were often characterized as mentally defective or psychopaths. Treatments for individuals exhibiting these traits varied from sterilization and castration to lobotomies and conversion therapy…Significant progress has been made in civil rights that have dramatically improved the legal protections available to this community, but challenges remain."

If there is a doubt that gay people are clear that much of their oppression has had to do with the views of so-called God-fearing people, the title of a 2009 anthology focused on the history of the gay liberation movement, edited by Tommi Avicolli Mecca, should remove that uncertainty. It was not called *Smash the Church, Smash the State* by accident.

The solution to the God Dilemma is, of course, not to "smash" anything, but to do just the opposite: to rebuild our society by writing a New Cultural Story, based around a totally different idea about a Higher Power.

# 19

Our species is being invited right now to decide—urgently invited, by the tide of events (the coronavirus outbreak of 2020 not the least among them)—what kind of God we want to believe in.

There are those who say that, given our present predicament, we would be better off to not believe in any kind of God; that there is no "Higher Power" at all. They would assert that our present beliefs have done more harm than good, and worse yet, that it's all been unnecessary, because the existence of an entity called "God" is pure myth.

Wherever you stand on this personally, we still, as a species, are faced with the God Dilemma—we still can't agree about who and what God is and what God wants. We still hold on to ideas about God that may be wildly inaccurate, ideas that aren't helping us create life on Earth in the way we all desire. If we want to change our daily experience, and the trajectory of life globally, something's got to give. The question is, what will it be?

Will we abandon our belief in God altogether? Or will we take a closer, honest look at our present hodgepodge of ideas about God and realize that if there *is* a Higher Power, we have so far totally squandered our opportunity to use it in a way that creates the collective reality for which we have so long yearned?

Will we then muster the courage to explore a new point of view about God that could cause us to be more loving as a species and more effective as producers of what we say we want the entire species to experience?

CRSO

The hypothesis here is that many people do not feel they've been given what they consider to be a truly viable *alternative* to the hodgepodge. Oh, they've all heard alternatives, for sure—but nothing the majority assess to be viable; nothing that it could enthusiastically, joyously, *unreservedly* adopt, accept, and apply as its new universally held belief about God.

Thus, many folks feel they're in an All or Nothing At All situation. Either they accept the fact that there are 4,300 separate religions in the world, each one explaining in no uncertain terms "what is so," or they throw their hands in the air and go with none.

They could, in the alternative, decide and declare that it is only *their* religion that has it right, and continue applying labels to the beliefs of others: blasphemy, apostasy, heresy, idolatry, heterodoxy, unorthodoxy, or simply inaccuracy and falsity.

This is, of course, what many people have been doing—and we see where it's taken us.

One would think that, with such a huge majority of us holding a belief in a Higher Power of *some* sort, our most natural course would be to opt for that closer, honest look, to see if there might be a totally different, and perhaps more accurate, understanding of God to be had—one that can be at least proposed as an hypothesis without massive objection, and perhaps even embraced one day without hesitation.

That is precisely what the New Definition Approach to the question of God offers. You will remember that it suggests this:

1   God can be referred to by many names—Energy, Essential Essence, Originating Source, etc.—but is perhaps best understood as Pure Love.

2   Pure Love is best defined as the energy that, when expressed, creates happiness in the sender and is sent with the intention of creating what the receiver also feels as happiness, allowing the receiver to respond freely and genuinely without losing the love being sent.

This invites the practitioner of Pure Love to follow the adage: "Speak your truth but soothe your words with peace." The beneficial impact that a collective embracing of this new way of being would have on the human race cannot, in my view, be overstated. I believe an immensely positive fallout would occur in all of our endeavors and experience.

To put this all into one sentence: Life would never be the same on Planet Earth.

Thank goodness.

Now, let me get specific...

# 20

Here's what could occur in some important areas of life—spirituality, relationships, and economics, to use three examples—should we collectively decide that God is Pure Love, and that so are we.

In the part of our human expression called Spirituality, I believe we would see these major shifts:

- Evidence of the acceptance and application of the new ethic arising out of the New Definition of Divinity would be visible everywhere.

- More and more religions would share that the Higher Power is not a bigger-than-life human-like entity, but rather, an energetic *essence* that is self-consciously aware of its Sacred and Singular Self, that is the consummate source of Wisdom and Intelligence, and that is undifferentiated in its Original State. It would be taught that Divinity has the ability to take on innumerable forms (including the life form of any sentient being in the cosmos) and can be thought of in any one of those forms.

- The use of what some would call "God Power" to produce material effects on Earth (a process once called, in some quarters, "alchemy," and more often now referred to as "manifestation") would become much easier and more consistently effective. This would be the result once the undifferentiated essence of Divinity is defined as a specific *feeling* that is familiar to humans and recognizable through sensory perception, and not simply an amorphous or nebulous "energy" without a particular characteristic, quality, or attribute. Our species could thus take much fuller advantage of the impact that a specific *type* of energy, intentionally directed, has upon energy itself.

- Most of the world's 4,300 religions would remain in place as cultural treasures of individual and generations-long customs, but all religions would hold as their First Teaching the elegant four-word message: God is Pure Love. This would unite the world's faith traditions, at last, under one overarching spiritual principal, opening the way for all the world's cultures and societies to embrace and practice a common ethic that would eliminate more than theological disagreements on Earth.

- There would arise among all people (who would now be joined together as a collective under an overarching spiritual principle) the recognition of a deep truth that creating the exterior reality of life is a collaborative process—something not widely taught previously.

(A wonderfully informative look at the whole Reality Creation Process is just ahead as we explore the mechanics—or, if you please, the metaphysics—of the New Definition Approach to understanding God.)

These are only some of the changes in our spirituality that I foresee. I am sure there would be more.

CRED

In that part of the human expression called Relationships, I believe we would see these major shifts occur:

- The purpose of relationships of every kind would be understood and experienced in an entirely different way. It would be clear that the true purpose of all relationships—distant relationships, business relationships, friendship relationships, familial relationships, romantically intimate relationships, relationships with pets, and relationships with all elements in Nature—has little to do with what can be gotten out of them, and everything to do with what can be put into them. Humans would know that their relationship with everything and everyone is the chief means by which every sentient being generates a direct experience of who they are and who they choose to be.

- It would be equally clear that this does not mean that endless giving in a relationship, to the detriment of one's own health or happiness, is the highest spiritual activity. To the contrary, it would be clear that *not* allowing one person to continually take advantage of another would be a very elevated form of love, in that it would stop such a person from experiencing and believing that their best or only way of being human is to require their own, and everyone else's, attention to be focused only on them. Failure to disapprove of or stop abusive behavior by another would be understood to actually be abusing to the abuser, allowing the abuser's behavior to continue until they themselves are injured by it.

- Romantic relationships would never end, in the way that people now use and understand the word "end." Rather, they would simply change form, and it would be understood that no relationship is ever terminated, but only altered in the way it is experienced.

- It would be understood by humans that every relationship which is allowed to become intimate on a physical level will carry with it a lasting concern and consideration for the other person's well-being, insofar as each person is capable of, and given the opportunity to be, lovingly supporting of the other on their life journey, even if they have taken a separate path.

- The fact of this lasting concern would not be experienced in anyone's life as a burden, or as producing a sense of obligation, but rather, as creating an opportunity for the voluntary expression of a soul's choice never to energetically abandon anyone who has ever been invited into the shelter of a deeply personal union.

- Relationships with inanimate objects—money, food, particular locations, articles of clothing, vehicles, souvenirs—would be understood to involve an exchange between two sources of energy, one self-aware and the other not, but both nevertheless made of the building blocks of Fundamental Essence. Humans would therefore acquire a reverence for everything in life—from plants to trees to oceans, shirts to shoes, cars to houses, stuffed toys to favorite pillows—having deeply understood the Ultimate Nature of Life Itself to be simply differing expressions and vibrations of the Single Energy of which all is comprised.

These are only some of the changes in our relationships that I foresee. I am sure there would be more.

∞

In that part of the human expression called Economics, I believe we would see these major shifts occur:

- The economic disparity that now exists, with the wealthiest one percent of people holding more than 50% of the world's total wealth—and with the richest one percent in the United States owning more wealth than the bottom 90%—would no longer be seen, even by those wealthiest folks, as an acceptable social profile in a world where 815 million people go to bed hungry every night. A voluntary sharing of wealth through free-will contributions to a global general fund dedicated to the most urgent needs of all human beings would be established and joyfully, fulfillingly maintained by those who have much, and who choose to make life better for those who have little.

- The corporate focus of the world's largest companies would shift from generating the highest possible profit to producing the highest possible benefit for the highest number of people that the company is capable of serving.

- The world's operative definition of "wealth" would change from a measure of cash and holdings to a measure of peace, joy, self-fulfillment, and love in one's life.

- Class divisions that formerly separated those who were called "the rich" from those who were called "the poor" would disappear.

- The payment of the lowest possible wages in order to produce the highest possible profits would be replaced by an entirely different business ethic that offered workers the greatest benefits practical and feasible in the operation of any business enterprise.

- Free access to the finest medical care, and availability of the best medicines, would be seen as a fundamental human right, paid for through the collection of voluntary cost-covering cash infusions from all people, proportionate to their income and holdings.

- No individual anywhere in the world would ever be required by circumstances to go without basic necessities of food, clothing, and shelter—much less starve to death or freeze to death.

These are only some of the changes in our economics that I foresee. I am sure there would be more.

CR&O

None of the above changes in any of these or other areas of our present reality are going to occur on a planetary scale if most of the human species stays where it is in its limited understanding of the Higher Power and of life, and of how we can all make God relevant in our experience.

Put plainly and simply, we're going to have to solve the God Dilemma. In our own personal lives first, and then, to the degree that life affords us the opportunity, in a way which touches those around us, and ultimately, the world at large.

# 21.

I ask your pardon for saying it a third time, but I'm going to declare definitively here that the time has come for all Idea Heroes to decide that enough is enough, that we're ready for our Collective Confusion to end, that we've paid sufficient homage to the 4,300 religions we have honored for centuries with our compliance, and that we are now going to invite every religion to speak with one voice, offering four words as their first shared teaching: God is Pure Love.

That's a pretty simple message, but its simplicity runs counter to how we've done everything we could think of on this planet to cause the whole subject of God to become one of the most complicated matters anyone could ever think of.

We've been looking for centuries for that single idea that could finally unite humanity and enhance our lives. We've tried political remedies, economic remedies, social remedies, and spiritual remedies of every kind.

Wouldn't it be interesting if some of us decided that our idea about God—which produces our ideas about life—need not be even a little complicated, because God is actually the simplest thing of all? Wouldn't it be interesting if *all of us* decided that?

I'm reminded of the first verse of the first song of the first performance of the first stage piece presented at the Kennedy Center for the Performing Arts in 1971. The production, titled *Mass,* was created by the American composer and conductor Leonard Bernstein on a commission from Jacqueline Kennedy, who asked him (a longtime friend) to write something special for the inaugural program of the magnificent building honoring her late husband.

I present those first few lyric lines here:

*Sing God a simple song*
*Lauda, Laudē*
*Make it up as you go along*
*Lauda, Laudē*

*Sing like you like to sing*
*God loves all simple things*
*For God is the simplest of all*

I was a member of the working press in those days and had the good fortune to be covering the event on that inaugural evening. I remember being touched at the deepest level when those words were sung to Maestro Bernstein's heart-opening music.

To this day I find myself affirming that wonderful insight. God *is* the simplest of all: Pure Love. Unconditional, unlimited, uncomplicated, unreserved and unambiguous. Wanting and needing nothing in return. Given simply for the sake and the joy of being expressed.

The solution to the God Dilemma is for us to move to that level of simplicity in our understanding of the Higher Power. Yet while we yearn to produce a civilization whose governmental decisions, economic constructions, and social interactions are based on a model of Pure Love, we don't seem to know how. And the *reason* we don't know how is what has been our stumbling block. It's our impediment, our hindrance, our insurmountable hurdle.

CRECD

And so yes, we are done, as well, with using as a model of Pure Love the old belief in the Biggest Model of All: a God who we are told does *not* model a love which demands nothing in return, but just the opposite.

Should we decide that God does *not* behave like this, but is a Deity who only expresses Pure Love, then we might be able to finally see ourselves doing the same. Especially if we focused on a *different* message from the book of Genesis, forgetting all the crazy stories about God slapping Cain in the face until Cain's face turned black.

We could decide that it is in Chapter 1, Verse 27 where Genesis has things right. That's where it says that humans are made in the image and likeness of God.

But could we have misunderstood even this seemingly straightforward message? Could we have interpreted this Bible passage to mean that as humans are, God is?

Is it possible that, having observed that humans *are*, in fact, judging and condemning, we assumed God must be like this, too, since we've been told that we were made in God's image and likeness? Have we unwittingly turned everything on its ear, and made God in the image and likeness of humans?

And could we have long held onto a second misunderstanding—that it's God's "job" to permit or not permit certain things to happen? Let's clarify that. As the coronavirus enveloped the Earth in 2020, many of God's faithful were asking, *How can a loving God allow this to happen?*

Let's tackle that head on right now.

# 22.

Is it "God's job" to fix everything? Does the Deity allow or disallow certain events in our lives?

No. I humbly offer that this is not so. It is not my truth that God is the Moment-to-Moment Caretaker of Humanity—even though many people seem to have cast God in that role in this movie called Our Life. And especially during parts of the "film" where unwelcome scenes are being played out, thousands find themselves asking, "Where is God in all of this?"

In the religion that I would create, it would be understood that God is not nodding "yes" or "no" to various options regarding what could or could not happen next on Earth. God would have no preference in the matter, even if God was given such a list of choices.

This is a tough one for many people to accept, this notion that God does not have an emotional investment in, nor approve or disapprove of, certain events, conditions, or circumstances arising in the experience of humans.

Here is where a large number of people might reject my idea of a good and workable religion, because it does drive back to the central question posed at the outset of this exploration on which we have embarked here: If God does not have a say in how our lives are turning out—or *want* things to turn out a certain way, for that matter—then what's the point of having a God at all? Why should it concern us at any level if a Supreme Being even exists, if it never intervenes in the affairs of humans?

So then, this information: The Supreme Being *does* intervene in the affairs of humans, but not in the way that we think, and not for the reasons that we imagine. God does not become involved in life on Earth because God feels that something is going wrong. God becomes involved in life on Earth if *we* feel something is going wrong, and we actively seek to use God to change it.

God's desire is to empower *us* to create what we wish to experience, not to tell us what *God* wants to experience. If it was the latter, humans would be nothing more than minions—servants, as it were—enslaved to a Deity who simply issues orders and punishes those who do not obey.

God's purpose, however, has not been to create a cosmic fiefdom, but rather, to experience the wonder and the glory of Divinity through the free expression of Its creations. God's "job," then, is to empower and encourage all sentient beings to experience the glory of who *they* are as expressions of The Whole.

If God is separately voting "yea" or "nay" on everything that is occurring, why would anything that we call "bad" ever happen? Obviously, God is not deliberately *choosing* for horrible things (by our definition) to occur, so how does it come to pass that they do? And since they clearly do, does this mean that God is Chairman of the Board of a world totally out of control?

No. What it does mean (to further utilize the metaphor) is that God has turned over control to the associates and colleagues who are actually running the company.

That means you and me.

God's Pure Love gives us total individual control over our inner response to outward events, and more collaborative control over the creation of those outward exterior events than we might have imagined.

Are there events that occur over which we have no control? Yes. An asteroid colliding with Earth might fall into that category. Yet are there many events—even major global geophysical events— which we say "just happened," that we could have avoided? Yes.

The fact that human beings have been gifted with Free Will gives them the ability to collectively produce events or circumstances of their choice (such as, for instance, the coronavirus outbreak), and then to live with the outcome.

CᴙℰϽ

*Oh, no, no, no, no, NO…you're not going to try to tell us that it was the human collective that created the coronavirus outbreak!…one* might now loudly protest. *One or two people, or a tiny handful, might have been involved in producing that, but not humanity as a whole!*

Well, actually…the pandemic wasn't the result of a single incident involving a small number of people and their actions in 2019. It was the result of the human race as a whole deciding, years before, what was important to us and what was not. That was our choice, that was our decision.

We were *told* that there was a *very high likelihood* of this kind of thing happening. We were given *notice*. And I'm talking about more than the short notice of a canary in a coal mine. I'm talking about warning after warning after warning, year after year after year, from scientist after scientist after scientist, about the possibility—actually, the *probability*—of our species thoughtlessly and carelessly creating the ideal conditions for a killer virus to emerge on this planet.

What I'm *not* talking about are warnings and pleadings that came to us too late. I'm talking about urgent calls *fifty years ago* for us to pay attention.

Did we listen? No. Our species moved forward with daily life, placing confidence in leaders who ignored those who were shouting alarms at the top of their lungs and waving red flags until they were exhausted.

It's about unpurified drinking water, they said. It's about improper use of antibiotics. Look at all the local warfare and its effects. Make note of the massive refugee migration. Please, please, *please*, they cried, pay attention to the changing social and environmental conditions around the world that are fostering the spread of new and potentially devastating viruses and diseases.

The wording above was inspired by a descriptive paragraph at Amazon.com about an important, nearly 30-year-old book titled *A Dancing Matrix: Voyages Along the Viral Frontier* by science writer Robin Marantz Henig.

Published in February 1993, the book's content is the centerpiece of an article by Ms. Henig appearing on NationalGeographic.com in April 2020 under the headline: *Experts warned of a pandemic decades ago. Why weren't we ready?*

Why, indeed. Twenty-seven years after her book was published, and *a half-century* after the warnings that she wrote about were issued, humanity was forced to confront its own unwitting complicity in the rapid and worldwide spread of the coronavirus in 2020.

No, we are not directly at cause in the matter, but it's undeniable that humanity could have done more, with preparation, to dramatically reduce the severity of the pandemic. But the species simply went stone deaf when people such as Nobel laureate Joshua Lederberg, an American molecular biologist, said things like: "The single biggest threat to man's continued dominance on the planet is the virus."

That statement appeared in the introduction to Ms. Henig's book. And it's not as if her text was our only warning. At least two other important books—*The Hot Zone* by Richard Preston and *The Coming Plague* by Laurie Garrett—were published in 1995, and *Spillover: Animal Infections and the Next Human Pandemic,* by David Quammen, was released *seven years before* the coronavirus hit.

Talk about a horn honking! And we still drove right into the middle of this intersection, oblivious to this "accident" waiting to happen. It's been said that forewarned is forearmed, but humanity has a way of not hearing what it does not want to hear—and then asking why *God* has allowed things like this to be visited upon us.

# 23

Seventeen-year-old Greta Thunberg spent much of 2019-2020 traveling to conference after conference and legislative assembly after assembly, urging and begging the world's leaders to take action in response to the climate crisis facing the earth—another thing that many national leaders have also been ignoring.

And our mutual blindness doesn't stop there. The world's tropical forests are disappearing at the rate of one football field's worth *every six seconds*, writers Jack Guy and Maija Ehlinger tell us in a June 2, 2020, story on CNN.

The day before, the same network carried a story by Ivana Kottasová which began: "The sixth mass extinction is not a worry for the future. It's *happening now, much faster* than previously expected, and it's *entirely our fault...*"

The story went on to say, "Humans have already wiped out hundreds of species and pushed many more to the brink of extinction through wildlife trade, pollution, habitat loss and the use of toxic substances. But the findings published in the scientific journal Proceedings of the National Academy of Sciences (PNAS) show that the rate at which species are dying out has accelerated in recent decades."

Scientists are telling us that microfibers and larger plastics from many other sources are polluting our oceans, badly degrading yet another critical planetary resource.

So if the planet's ecosystem undergoes irreversible damage, will we once again fall back on asking, *Why would a loving God allow such things?* Or will we see that it is *we* who are doing the allowing?

What *God* is doing, it's clear to me, is allowing *us* to do as we wish. God is also allowing us to *not* do what we *don't* do or *won't* do. To reiterate, the function of The Divine is not to protect us from ourselves, but to empower us to project ourselves into the universe as the species we wish to be, defined by the choices and decisions we make.

But what about geophysical events? Are we not, at least in these instances, absolved of any and all responsibility? Not in every case, actually. How many underground nuclear weapons tests do we think we can conduct before the massive explosions we produce loosen or dislodge the interconnecting plates that form the substructure of the planet's undergirding, eventually resulting in more earthquakes and tidal waves than the natural course of events might have ever produced?

How much carbon can we emit before we overload the earth's natural greenhouse mechanism and cause significant warming of the planet, such that the rising temperatures of its massive waters produce geothermal conditions generating wind variations violent enough to call them hurricanes and tornadoes?

While we are doing all of these things, does it make sense for us to ask: "Why would a loving God allow these earthquakes and tornadoes and hurricanes to increase like this?"

Would Earth be a better place if we had simply listened to the virus warnings of 50 years ago? Will it be a better place if we listen *now* to the warnings about our environment?

Will we see fewer tragic geophysical events on the planet if we stop blowing it apart from the inside, and stop contaminating the air with pollutants and the water with plastic and other contaminants on the outside?

We might do well to listen to the words of newspaper columnist George F. Will, who wrote in a June 2020 opinion piece for the Washington Post: "In life's unforgiving arithmetic, we are the sum of our choices."

CRED

Pure Love can be much more than simply a new definition of God. My intention here has not been to merely place before you a new idea about the Deity. I'd like you to walk away with a *tool*, not just an *idea*.

Pure Love can be not only a new way of living. It can also be a new way of focusing the Essential Energy as a powerful tool for change. But we have to know how to utilize it.

As I said earlier, eight out of ten of us may agree that a Higher Power exists, but I'm betting that only two out of ten of us *use that power intentionally, consistently, and constructively.*

That is largely because most people are not familiar with the *mechanics* of how to apply that Higher Power to everyday life. So that's where we're going next, as we render our exploration of a New Definition Approach to understanding God functional, and not just conceptual.

# PART II

## *The Mechanics*

# 24.

If we're going to talk about Pure Love as an energy, and if we're going to say that this particular energy is what God *is*, then an explanation of how to *use* that energy, how to direct it and project it, would be most beneficial now.

We haven't said much so far about the specifics of how to *engage* this New Force for Change in our day-to-day lives, but let's do so now. We need to look at not just the *model* of Pure Love, but the *mechanics* of it; not just the *energy*, but the *engine*; not just the *promise*, but the *process*.

I am talking now about what may be for many people the developing of a new skill. In fact, I believe that humanity as a whole is fast approaching what I consider to be the final frontier.

In a word: metaphysics.

We've already noted that this is not an aspect of life that has been widely understood by the human species. The term itself is not widely understood. It emerges from the philosophies of Aristotle and was understood to refer to that which comes *after* physics in our learning process. That is, first we learn about the physical world—what it is and how it functions—then we learn about the *meta* (loosely translated from the Greek as "after") physical world...which is the *cause* of the physical world.

We humans have actually learned about "cause and effect" *in reverse order*. First, we saw the effect...we observed what was happening...and only then did we explore the cause. We wanted to know *why* what was happening *was* happening *the way* it was happening.

"Metaphysics" could thus be described as *the "Why" of Life*. This is what makes it so powerful—and so dangerous if engaged unconsciously. To use a metaphor, we're playing with matches in the dynamite room. Then we're wondering why things are blowing up all around us.

So perhaps a Short Course in Metaphysics might be timely here.

☙❧

It is my awareness that what God has created is a *process*, an intricate system of singular energetic vibrational emanations that produce the characteristics of all physical objects. These objects generate energy exchanges in a cause-and-effect relationship that produces events in the physical realm.

This process is the cause of all things, and it is a process in which we are all continually involved, since we are all both senders and receivers of energy.

Now, this important detail: *Ideas* are energetic vibrational emanations. *Intentions* are energetic vibrational emanations. *Conceptualizations* are energetic vibrational emanations. All of these are forms of *thought,* and *thoughts* can be measured. Detected. *Felt.* And projected.

All physical objects and life forms, not just human beings, react to the energy exchanges going on in life all the time. Did you ever walk into a room where "the air was so thick you could cut it with a knife?" Sure, you have. We all have. Nobody has to say anything. No one even has to have a particular expression on their face. You can *feel* the tension *in the air*.

Likewise, when the energy of the moment is uplifting and positive, it can be felt by people just entering the space.

Being touched by the energy exchanges all around them, sentient beings are able to then respond from their Mind and Soul in a way which expresses their understanding, knowing, and choice about Who They Are and how they choose to experience any given moment.

Reduced to one sentence: Everything is comprised of energy, and everything exudes or radiates energy towards everything else.

We see, then, that everything has an *impact* on everything else. It may be a very small impact—in some cases, negligible— or it may be a significant impact, depending upon who or what is projecting the energy, and how many sources are projecting it in the same direction in the same way at the same time.

The impact of your energy and mine can be substantial. This is because all sentient beings such as us have the ability to consciously create both the *type* of energy they project (positive or negative), and the *intensity* of that energy.

We do this by deliberately choosing the emotion we wish to express in a given situation. Not all life forms have this capability.

To illustrate this difference: turtles do not become angry. Neither do snakes. You can't make a snake mad or scared. It reacts to exterior events or conditions based on instinct, not emotion. A lion, on the other hand, can be angered and afraid. Trust me on this. You don't want to test this out.

A lion is not, however, prone to introspection. It is difficult to imagine a lion sitting around after roaring a territorial invader away and thinking, "Gee, I wonder if I roared a bit too loud there. Could I have overreacted? I need to watch that. What will the other lions think?"

Humans can also be angered or scared, but unlike other life forms on this planet, humans make value judgments—weighing their actions against certain philosophies and particular ideas, specific concepts and, sometimes, theological constructions—and often *changing their mind* about being angry or afraid, and deciding to be just the opposite—even as their very survival is being threatened.

The marvelous anecdote about an incident in the life of author Byron Katie comes to mind here. Author Jim Dreaver wrote about this on his website (JimDreaver.com):

"This story was told to me by a friend who heard it directly from Stephen Mitchell, Byron Katie's husband...Byron Katie and Stephen were walking back to their car late at night, when a man suddenly slipped out of the darkness, grabbed Byron Katie by the shoulder, stuck a gun in her face, and said: 'Give me everything you've got or I'm gonna kill you!'

"Without missing a beat, Bryon Katie turned to him, and in a calm voice said: 'I wouldn't do that, sweetie...You'll just create a terrible mess for yourself.' At which point, the would-be mugger released his grip on her and fled back into the darkness!

"Now *that* is the embodiment of true presence, true fearlessness!"

What gives humans the ability to make the kind of choice that Byron Katie made is a deliberate decision, entered into *ahead of time,* to remain fully conscious of the choices that each moment in life places before us.

This is a perfect example of how to use metaphysics in a positive and powerful way.

The fact is that most of us encounter our life's choices unconsciously. The result is that, more often than not, we act out of herd instinct. This does not always produce the best result.

(And that, my friends, is the understatement of the year.)

But there's a way out of this behavioral trap. And your escape is easier than what you may think.

I mean that literally. Read the sentence again. Your escape has little to do with what you may think, and everything to do with what you may choose as your next projected emotion. Will it be a conscious choice or an unconscious choice?

What emotion are you choosing to project right now, in this moment, as you are reading this? Excitement or boredom? Interest or disinterest? Enthusiasm or restiveness? Are you choosing your emotion *consciously* or *unconsciously?* Is it being intentionally created by you, or is it just falling over you?

These are the two ways in which metaphysics comes into play as a practical matter when we make decisions in our daily lives. And *deliberately* projected emotion is metaphysics of the first rank, of the highest order.

We are making decisions all the time, of course. Big decisions, little decisions, important choices, unimportant choices, selections that matter, selections that don't matter. What does matter is whether you know you're doing this—and know *when* you are doing it. What is important is that you are aware that the power is always on.

Not *when* the power is on, but *that* the power is on.

You are experiencing an emotion and making a decision out of it, right now about whether to even continue reading this book. That decision could affect the rest of your life.

# 25.

When using metaphysics, it's critical to know that there are two categories into which all energetic projections fall:

**1**  Collective vs. Individual

**2**  Conscious vs. Unconscious

Let's look at that first category, because this is where the greatest misunderstanding lies, as I observe it.

Many spiritual teachers, lecturers and authors have been making a very misleading statement through the years. They have said: "You create your own reality." And they leave it at that.

This declaration has produced one of the most often mistaken notions that people hold about how reality is created. The announcement has left many with the impression that we are each producing, individually, the events of our own lives.

Some have taken it to mean that we have created everything that's happened not only in our own life, but in the lives of those around us. Our spouse. Our children. Our Uncle Joe falling down last week and spraining his ankle, canceling his much-looked-forward-to visit with us. Our boss, suddenly confronted with an illness and having to close down her business, leaving us without a job. The woodlands fire season upending our nation. Racial injustice upending our peace. A virus upending our world.

Did we create that? Did our uncle or our boss create that? Where does our responsibility begin and where does it end?

It is important to see that not even from a metaphysical point of view are we individually creating everything that has happened, or will happen, in our life. Not in the way that many of us may have been led to understand.

The exterior events of physical life are being created co-jointly by all of us. It is our interior emotional response to those events that we are creating individually. And *that* is what is meant by the teaching: "You create your own reality."

Now that may seem obvious to most, but it is not as clear to everyone as one might think. Because of the misleading, incomplete way that the truth "you create your own reality" has been passed on by many teachers, some people fall into what I call New Age Guilt when things occur that they do not welcome.

They ask themselves, "Now, why would I create that?", and in their upset over what's occurred, they admonish themselves for not using their powers of creation more mindfully.

This actually happened to me in my life. I was attending one of those classes that you could find everywhere back in the 80s about how to use "mind power" to change your life. And the instructor did, in fact, say: "You create your own reality." So I got the definite impression that as I think, so will it happen.

Then I had an interesting experience. I was attending a "new age" church in those days that featured a minister who spoke endlessly about how we generate reality. After the Sunday service one week, while having coffee and a donut in the church's fellowship hall, a friend in the congregation casually asked me, "How's it going?" I answered honestly with, "You know, things aren't so good at work right now. I think something's up. My boss is starting to sound like he's unhappy with me." And my friend said, "Well, why are you creating that?"

I remember chuckling to myself and thinking that I wanted to do was reply, "I don't know. Why are *you* creating *this?*"—and punch him in the nose. Of course, I didn't do that. But it got me wondering: Who is responsible for what, in a creation that involves more than one person (which nearly all of them do)?

A couple of months later I was, in fact, laid off. And yes, I caught myself reprimanding myself for "creating" that.

Then I ran into my old boss at a local shopping center a few days later and I found myself having to say, "Tell me, what did I do wrong that made you fire me?" He looked surprised, then replied, "Wrong? You didn't do anything wrong. We've simply hit a rough patch financially, and I had to do what I had to do, which was to cut staff. You were our most recent hire, so it was simply a case of seniority. I had to go with 'last in, first out.' I'm really sorry it happened that way. You were really very good, and we hated to lose you."

Ah! So he did what served *his* agenda! I had nothing to do with it, in the way that I was imagining.

So who created the rough patch for my boss' company? Did I create that, or did he create that? Or did his clients create that by not spending as much money with him? *Who creates what? Or are we all creating everything together?*

This was an important awakening for me. I saw clearly that, yes, we're creating the exterior events in our life collaboratively, each of us experiencing individually the collectively-produced occurrence, as the next step in our own evolutionary process. But thinking that I was "doing this all to myself" was neither accurate, nor metaphysically beneficial.

Coming to that kind of conclusion can have a real-time impact on one's life, because the way we respond interiorly to any immediate exterior circumstance can often affect the way those exterior circumstances play out.

My initial self-recrimination about my "mis-use" of life's creative energy did not make it easier for me to feel positive about "where to from here." It was finding out a few days later that I did not actually "create" losing my job through my negative thinking that helped me to rearrange my internal energy around being out of work—and I actually found a new job within a week as I came to embrace that I was *good* at what I do.

To summarize all of metaphysics in 11 words: *The energy of life is affected by the energy of life.*

What is projected *from* us is injected *by* us into whatever is *before* us—whether it's in our mind or physically present in our exterior environment. If we project the energy of resistance into the energy of any unwelcome exterior event or circumstance, we give it strength by empowering its originating vibration.

CRED

Does this mean we should not seek to change something that arises in our exterior experience if we disagree with it? No. Of course not. It actually means just the opposite. It means that we're invited to use a much more powerful *tool* of change. Not resistance, but love.

If we pour love into all that is arising (as described in Chapter 11), we have suddenly and dramatically harnessed the most powerful energy in the universe. We then stand a far better chance of affecting that with which we disagree, and in a way that more closely matches that which we prefer and desire. And if *two or more* use life's most powerful energy in this way, miracles can occur.

Remember this always: In the world of energetics, negativity only breeds negativity. As well, positivity breeds positivity. Much will depend on how many people are holding a particular kind of energy with regard to the exterior circumstances or events of life. If you live in an environment in which most people's first emotion is negative, most people's first experience will be negative.

A more positive interior energetic response can also bring one to a place of true inner peace and genuine internal serenity, no matter how the exterior circumstance created by the multitude continues to present itself. And peace and calmness, alone, can often dramatically alter one's interior experience of any moment in life.

# 26.

I said that there are two categories into which all energetic projections fall:

1  Collective vs. Individual
2  Conscious vs. Unconscious

Looking at that second category, it is true that humanity has the ability to create its own reality, but most often this ability is being engaged unconsciously. That is, without an awareness that we are doing it. The result: half of what we're creating, we are creating accidentally.

In this regard, there is one circumstance in particular to look out for. What people are *not* paying attention to is just as powerful as what they *are* paying attention to. So it is helpful to remember this: *Not to decide is to decide.*

The act of doing nothing is just as powerful as the act of doing something, especially if the nothing we are doing follows something we have already done. If you drop a glass on the floor, but do nothing to pick up the shards, your bare feet will pay a price tomorrow.

Whether it's creating the conditions that produced the perfect environment for a global viral outbreak, contributing to the frequency of earthquakes and tidal waves with underground nuclear tests, or the continued use of fossil fuels as our main source of energy on a planet whose natural elements (sun, wind and waterfalls) could supply sufficient energy to meet half of the world's power needs without using a drop of oil, we've looked the other way and decided to do little or nothing about the shards on the floor.

(We still don't put solar panels on every home or building, even though we've had the capability for well over half a century. We still don't put electric cars in every driveway, even though the first successful one was built in 1891, and modern versions can travel 245 miles on a single charge.)

So ignoring what we're doing is one form of unconscious energy projection. The text here has offered some striking examples of this.

Another form of unconscious energy projection is allowing initial thoughts to determine emotions. If our first thoughts about an event or circumstance are either not accurate or not the most generous, we could unconsciously generate emotions which, because of their nature and intensity, produce outcomes we might not intentionally choose.

The biggest reason that so much of our creation is unconscious is that the process of creation is working all the time, whether we want it to or not. The power switch is always on.

The question is not *whether* every element in life is affected by every other element, but how *great* is the effect, and if there is any way we can control or direct it. That's what metaphysics is all about.

Our emotion creates our energy projection. Our individual emotion projection creates our inward reality of every collectively created outward event or circumstance. The more that our emotion joins with and matches those of others, the more we create our collective outer experience.

It is not an accident that sports teams perform better, and generally win more often, in front of home crowds than in the stadiums of their opponents. This is so widely understood that it is routinely referred to as the "home field advantage."

Understanding how energy works helps us more and more to avoid the unconscious use of metaphysics. We know now how powerfully what we did *not* do 50 years ago about the virus threat wound up affecting the entire planet beginning in 2020. Will this inspire us to pay more emotional attention to the ecology crisis looming before us now, and which could create another truly global calamity if we do not?

Time will tell.

Each of us, for sure, can reduce the amount of unconscious creation in which we engage in our personal lives and, by extension, in our world, by staying awake to what emotions we are creating within us each day.

Most of us seek to change any unwelcome outward reality only when we decide we have had just about enough. Yet in an Advanced Civilization we would use our emotions long before that time, not to *protect*, but to *produce*. Not to shield us from what we are facing, but to generate and create what we *wish* to face.

In short, we would *create* our emotion, rather than *have* an emotion. We would decide beforehand how we choose to feel about something, and we would pour that feeling all over what we are currently confronting and then deciding about.

This is something that many people do not fully understand: Emotions are energies we *decide* to experience, not energies to which we are *subjected*. Human emotions are deliberately chosen, not unintentionally encountered. They do not arise from some place outside of our control. Emotions are, in the purest sense of the words, creations, not reactions.

When something occurs in our exterior world, we *decide* in our interior world how we want to be with regard to it. Do we want to be sad; do we want to be angry, do we want to be happy, do we want to be totally okay or totally not okay? We make this decision, and then we find ourselves "being" that.

I do know that many people would say that emotions "just come up" for them in response to events and circumstances. They might put it this way: "I'm sorry, I just get emotional over stuff like this." But what I have come to understand is that the mind works lightning fast. It analyzes incoming data, compares it to all previously stored data, and decides what's "true" about what is happening. It then turns that "truth" into a thought about who we are and how we wish to experience ourselves next, choosing to express a particular emotion as a means of putting all that energy into motion.

This all happens, as I said, very quickly. We're talking about milliseconds. So yes, it can often feel as if we really have been "overcome" with emotion. But our response arises out of a fully conscious *decision-making* process nonetheless.

Once we acknowledge this and apply that awareness in our lives, we have stepped onto the path to mastery. We can choose love over fear, peace over unrest, tranquility over anger, joy over sorrow, and positivity in all its forms over negativity in any form.

CR80

The wonder of actively and consciously choosing emotions that we wish to experience in certain kinds of moments is that we can, in fact, make these choices ahead of time. Byron Katie may never have thought she'd come face-to-face with a mugger and may not have prepared for that moment specifically. But I feel certain she knew that she'd come face-to-face with situations that could bring fear into her life, and that she made a conscious decision about which emotion she chooses to express when confronted with the opportunity to express fear. She then invokes that choice when the opportunity to express fear actually arises.

We do not have to wait until something in particular occurs to make such decisions. Because life is repetitive, we can decide now that "the next time this happens…(the next time I lose my keys, the next time the hotel doesn't have my reservation, the next time someone is a half-hour late, or even, the next time I'm in danger)…I'm going to create the following emotion…"

We can also choose to forget our emotions altogether—to not "get emotional" at all—by sidestepping the Mind and going right to the Soul. We can decide to not choose *our* emotion but choose instead to express how God would feel in any situation. Or we can make them both the *same*.

It is when we meld the two that the most powerful creation begins. For it is in those moments that we take the most valuable tool out of our metaphysical toolbox and begin to build an experience called Mastery in Living.

We're discussing this in-depth here because the important thing in metaphysics is to translate concept into function, to turn explanation into application.

It's all very nice to redefine God as Pure Love, and to understand that emotion creates energy that can affect outcomes, but if we're not using emotion for that purpose, our New Definition Approach to understanding the Higher Power winds up being only a conceptualization. There's nothing functional about it.

It was in Chapter 4 that the following question was posed: "If there *is* a Higher Power, and we're simply not using it effectively, wouldn't that be a shame? Wouldn't it be a terrible waste?"

I am asserting here that this is exactly the case.

The challenge has been that, in the past, most of the world's religions encouraged followers to obtain God's help by asking for it through prayer. This presumes that God is an Outside Source (rather than a Source residing within them).

This construct relegated believers to hoping that the Higher Power *agreed* to honor their request, and with their level of deservedness in having it be granted. Doubts about either could reduce the power of the output of their metaphysical energy. Pleading is never as powerful as commanding.

Commanding? We're supposed to *command God?* In a sense, yes. We're not really giving God "orders," we're actually following God's orders. We have been told to *declare* what we want God to do ("Give us this day our daily bread."), not ask God to do it ("Please, could you give us some bread today?")

The idea is to experience yourself as *containing* an energy that has been gifted to us by God, thus changing the interaction with the Divine from a *request* to a *decree*.

When we gratefully *proclaim* what is so, rather than hopefully *plead* for it to be so, we use the Divine energy of Pure Love in the way it was designed to be used. We can do this by *loving the outcome before it occurs.*

# 27.

We're going to close this exploration of how to solve the God Dilemma with a look at a very effective formula that can help us to love all outcomes in life before they occur, and thus use metaphysics purposefully, beneficially and *intentionally*, rather than accidentally.

The moment you imagine any possible negative outcome that occur in any possible circumstance in your life, *love it to death*. I could almost say I mean that literally. Kill off the negative energy with love. Cut it off at the pass. Snip it in the bud.

How? With one magical component of energy projection that must, must, *must* be mentioned in every discourse on the subject, and I've saved it for last because of its importance. It really is magical.

You are engaging Pure Love, and what I call Masterful Metaphysics, when you consciously call *forth* the God Energy that is within you, rather than call *for* it to be with you. You can use this energy to respond to something that is occurring in this moment, or project it toward producing something that you would like to occur in some future moment.

The process begins as you consider a situation, circumstance, or event in your life and consciously adjust any emotion that your mind creates, to perfectly match the feeling of the soul (the feeling of the soul *being* God's feeling, since the soul is an Individuation of Divinity).

This is the deliberate melding of your emotion with God's feeling that we've been looking at here. But when this idea was first introduced, we did not explore how to *project* that coalesced energy of Pure Love into the Contextual Field.

Here's how that can be done: Metaphysical projection is often best achieved by "feeling into" whatever you wish to affect in a positive way. Put simply, allow yourself to experience the emotion that you imagine you would experience if the outcome you desire was already manifest in your reality.

Now here comes the magic ingredient. The most powerful emotion I would experience if an outcome I desired was already manifest in my reality would be: Gratitude.

Gratitude is not merely an emotion; it is a decision. So powerful is this decision that it becomes a definition, telling us "what is so" about any situation, circumstance, or event.

Many people are not aware of the immense power of Gratitude to reverse a thought that is at the foundation of all suffering. The central cause of suffering is the idea that something is happening that should not be happening. Gratitude unleashes an energy that turns this idea on its head, announcing that just because something may be unpleasant does not mean it is unbidden, unwelcome, or unwanted.

Pain (both physical and emotional) is a good example. It can, in fact, be welcome for any one of a number of reasons (childbirth, tooth extraction, or the end of an extremely difficult relationship, among them.)

The screech of an in-home smoke alarm can also be welcome, even if it is unpleasant. Seeing that your car has a flat tire just as you were about to get in and drive off can be unpleasant, but a very welcome event when you think about what life could have been like had the tire gone flat while you were doing 65 on the freeway. Failing to get the job or the promotion you applied for can be unpleasant, unless you use it to fortify your determination to never give up, bringing you the next job or advancement, and leading to you moving forward with a very successful career.

I want to come closer to home with this. The fragrance of my father's cigar was never very pleasant to me, but oh, how I'd welcome it now if it meant he was standing nearby, which he hasn't been for 30 years.

So something being unpleasant does not necessarily or automatically mean it must be unwelcome. If, on the other hand, the mind holds a thought that a particular experience is totally not okay with you, your mind will not abide it—and you will be tempted to produce an emotion that creates struggle in your life, and suffering.

It is Gratitude that could cause you to change your mind.

Yet Gratitude is not a tool with which to fool the mind, it is a tool with which to open the mind. It expands your normal, limited thinking to include a counter-intuitive truth: even when something seems "bad" for you, it can actually be good for you.

More than a tiny handful is the number of people who have experienced what they thought, in a particular moment, was one of the worst things that could ever happen to them, only to come to know later that it was one of the *best* things that ever happened. The Masterful Metaphysician is the one who realizes this *ahead of time*.

And we've already talked about how *everything* that occurs is to our benefit, in the sense that it leads to our continuing evolution. Even tragic events in life do so.

CRE0

As Individuations of Divinity, we are all invited to train the mind to move into gratitude in as many moments as we can—even if we encounter, initially, exactly the opposite of what we are desiring.

May I give you an example of how this could work in "real life"?

A few years ago, I was faced with a major challenge. My heart was failing. I realized there was a major problem when I could hardly carry a bag of groceries in from the car without huffing and puffing and needing to sit down for twenty minutes to regroup.

I was also feeling occasional discomfort in my chest. So I couldn't kid myself any longer that I was "just getting old." I clearly needed to see a cardiologist. One examination and he immediately recommended an angiogram. One look at the results of that and he immediately recommended open-heart surgery. "This is not elective," he said.

"And we're not talking about within the next six months. We're talking about within the next six weeks."

He said the angiogram had revealed severe blockages in several of the main arteries to my heart. "You need a triple… maybe even a quadruple bypass, and you need it right now."

This was not the greatest news of my life, nor was it the most eagerly anticipated event of my year. As I began contemplating this new turn of events, I started by doing something that always brings me comfort, which is saying my favorite prayer:

"Thank you, God, for helping me to understand that this problem has already been solved for me."

Then I encouraged myself to move into gratitude as I looked at exactly what was going on. First, I considered the fact that I had been given enough warning to seek out help. Secondly, I felt thankful that the subsequent input I received was so beneficial.

And thirdly, I was being admitted to one of the finest cardiac care facilities on America's west coast, that just so happens to be located in the valley in which I live. Finally, and I'd been placed in the hands of a man I'd learned was among the most highly skilled cardiovascular surgeons—and he just happened to have time on his surgery schedule to accommodate my suddenly arising need.

It turned out, by the way, that I did not need a triple bypass or a quadruple bypass. I needed a *quintuple* bypass. During surgery it was discovered that a fifth artery was nearly 90% blocked. To put it in my cardiologist's post-procedure words, "You were a walking time bomb."

I recall the moments before the operation as if this all happened yesterday. I felt inordinately calm, lying there on the gurney and squeezing my wife's hand before they gently told her they had to get me into the Prep Room. I whispered, "Everything will be alright. I love you," and they wheeled me away.

Lying alone, waiting to be taken into the operating suite, I again entered a space of deep gratitude, thinking to myself, "Thank you, God. No matter how this turns out, it'll be perfect. I'll either continue in my life over here feeling much better, or I'll be coming home to you. Gosh, I can't lose!" I remember actually feeling excited in a peacefully joyful way.

I've used gratitude in this way in moments of lesser import as well: running late getting to the airport, missing an important call, losing data that I thought for sure I'd just saved on my computer…unwelcome events, large and small, that in my younger years would have caused consternation.

I notice it's possible to project the energy of gratitude into any situation. I've trained myself to appreciate the good that I know arises from every situation. For me, it's a matter of using imagery and feeling.

First, I visualize an important event in my mind. It could be a past occurrence, or something I'm anticipating. Then I encourage myself to actually "feel the feeling" of thankfulness for it, either through noticing that the past event is over and I've evolved in my spiritual understanding because of it, or by creating a short "movie" in my mind of a future event turning out exactly the way I want it to.

When I say that I've trained myself to "appreciate" the good, I mean that I make both the good, and my awareness of it, *bigger*. As a property "appreciates" in value, so does the good in every circumstance grow bigger through the process of "appreciation."

Now I don't want to suggest for a moment that I've become the model of patience and imperturbability as I move through the minutia of each day ("Darn it! Now where is that mayonnaise!?!"). But I will say that when the big waves hit, I don't find myself emotionally swept away by them anymore. And even in many of life's smaller moments I'm getting better and better. ("Oh, my honey *didn't* hide it from me. It's right there behind the mustard!")

∞

I mentioned a moment ago what I call the Contextual Field. This is a phrase I use to describe the aspect of metaphysics that provides a context which allows particular expressions of life to be experienced.

I cannot experience that which is "big," for instance, without that which is "small" being known to me. I cannot experience that which is "fast" without that which is "slow" being known to me. I cannot experience that which is "smooth" without that which is "rough" being known to me.

So opposites are integral parts of our arena of activity, and they will arise in our awareness whenever we use metaphysics to create something. We actually energetically *call them into our awareness* the moment we choose to experience any particular facet of life or of who we are. They do not have to appear as part of our localized or in-the-moment experience, however. The awareness that they exist is sufficient. Even a memory of them serves their purpose.

The existence of opposites is a great gift to us and is an automatically arising feature of the metaphysical process of creation.

Therefore, when the opposite of what you seek to manifest arises in your awareness, express gratitude for this arising, for your gratitude demonstrates that you know exactly what's happening right now. Namely, that the groundwork is in place making it possible for you to experience what you have called forth. More important, the positive vibrational emanation affects the Contextual Field, building the energetic signature of what you choose to *have* happen.

All of this is what makes gratitude like magic.

And there is a final note I'd like to leave you with in this exploration. It explains your very reason for living.

# 28

Ultimately, as you achieve a new level of mastery in being human, you will notice that what you wish to experience, in the end, often has very little to do with the physical elements in life, and everything to do with its metaphysical elements.

Your highest desire will not center on the having or doing of something, but rather, the being of something. You will yearn to be more understanding and more loving, to be more caring and compassionate, to be even more generous and giving, to be humorous and light-hearted and welcome in everyone's home. In short, you will yearn to demonstrate Divinity. You will want to experience, through the expression of it, Who You Really Are.

You will realize that it has been in moments when you have achieved this in the past that you have felt fulfilled. The experience is one of pure bliss—which is the inevitable effect of Pure Love having been projected by you into your environment.

This approach to life can change your priorities overnight. It would change the entire planet in the blink of an eye if the largest number of us adopted these priorities. To use a metaphor, it would totally upset the apple cart.

We have been told that Survival is humanity's fundamental instinct. This is an inaccurate piece of information, yet that's the apple cart as it's presently set up. We've passed on this false axiom from generation to generation, allowing it to dictate far too many of our individual and collective, local and global, minor and major decisions throughout the history of our species.

If Survival were the Basic Instinct, we would not run into the burning building.

Let me explain. Imagine that a person is walking down the street and suddenly notices that a building off to the left is on fire. "Oh, my God!" they exclaim, and in the next instant they hear a baby crying from inside the building. Now, does that person stand there and *think about things?* Do they weigh the odds? ("Let's see…if I run in there, I could get caught in the flames. I might not even find that baby. Gee, I wonder what the odds are that I can survive this…")

No, of course not. Psychological studies have shown that the average person would race into the building immediately, with no thought for their personal safety. This is because humanity's fundamental instinct is not *survival*—it is the *expression of Divinity*. The question in that moment is not whether you're going to live or die, but *how* you're going to live or die. And that question answers itself in the blink of an eye, precisely because the response is *instinctive*.

Now the secret to life is to *see every moment as a Burning Building Moment*. The secret to being able to express Pure Love in your life is to follow your *real* Basic Instinct: the expression of your True Identity.

When you change your life's priorities to be all that you truly are, you will have engaged at last the Agenda of the Soul. You will have remembered your reason for living. And you will have remembered the truth about Divinity—which is that God gives all and requires nothing in return.

CRS

You have solved the God Dilemma. And deep inside, you are clear that every other dilemma in your life—and even every other human-made problem on Earth—could also be resolved, if enough of us were to decide that God is Pure Love, that we are Pure Love, and that all it takes to change our individual lives and the world is to *demonstrate* Pure Love.

That will, I assure you, upset the apple cart, because it will pull the underpinning from humanity's current political, economic, social, and spiritual rationalizations for our whole way of living.

It is for this reason that I have urged people to upset those carts in a peaceful, nonviolent, but clear and intentioned manner, whenever and wherever they can.

Apple-cart-upsetting is not something that many people on this planet like to see done. They don't want anyone tampering with their most sacred beliefs. Never mind that those constructions and religious dogmas have done little to produce a world free of hatred, violence, and fear. Never mind that those moral values and teachings about God have failed to eliminate suffering, reduce abject poverty, or even do something as simple as end hunger on our planet.

Even if their beliefs are clearly and demonstrably ineffective in producing the outcomes they are intended to produce, most human beings cling to those beliefs with a stubborn rigidity that is both shocking and appalling.

For instance, did you know that—paleontological and archaeological discoveries of the past quarter century notwithstanding—surveys show that over 40% of this planet's population continue to believe that the world is no more than ten thousand years old?

People believe what they want or need to believe in order to support their previously held point of view. In a startling number of instances, it truly is a case of "don't bother me with the facts." Nowhere is this in greater evidence than in our 4,300 religions.

We know what we know about God and we don't want to hear anything else. And there's a powerful reason for this. I've pointed it out explicitly and unambiguously in this book's narrative. Our thoughts about God form the bedrock of our entire understanding of Life.

*That is why the God Dilemma is no small thing.*

Yet even though many, many people agree that our species has still not gotten its act together around the question of a Higher Power after hundreds of thousands of years, a *solution* to the God Dilemma may not even be welcome. Why? Because it could be the Great Apple Cart-Upsetter of all time, for many agnostics, atheists, and adherents alike.

Since most people want to leave their religious beliefs alone, we find ourselves insisting on building a life in the first quarter of the 21st century with first century spiritual tools.

In medicine, this would be like trying to perform surgery with a very sharp stick. In technology, it would be like trying to send a rocket to the moon with the spark of a flint stone. In science, it would be like trying to conduct an experiment in the dim light from an opening of a cave.

Still, leaving our religious beliefs untouched could make sense if those tools were working. But we are not allowed to even *question* if they're working. The problem is not with the tools, we tell ourselves, the problem is that not enough people are using them.

Yet a keen observer would realize that the problem is exactly the opposite. The problem is that we *are* using them. And we're using them against each other. Thus, the tools of our ancient religions have proven ineffective (to put it mildly) in creating a world of peace, harmony, sufficiency, and dignity for all.

So we end this book with the same question with which we began: What is wrong here?

It's a question we're not supposed to ask. We're supposed to keep doing the same thing over and over again, expecting to get a different result. And that, of course, is the classic definition of insanity.

Like a fly against a windowpane, we keep banging our head against that which we do not see—or, in our case, which we refuse to see: that there must be something fundamentally flawed in our current beliefs about God, about Life, and about ourselves, or we would be way past where we are now in our social and spiritual development.

So the inquiry that arises is: Are we willing to consider the possibility that there may be something we do not fully understand about God, about Life, and about Who We Are—the understanding of which would change everything?

Are we willing to consider new ideas, new thoughts, new constructions within the human story, even if they seem on the surface to contradict what we think we already know about God and Life? Can we at least explore their possibilities?

The explorations here have offered you an opportunity to do just that. The suggestion is that one thing we can do that could (if enough of us do it) help change the course of humanity's future, is to encourage the adoption of a new ethic for our species.

We are talking about a new personal ethic, a new business ethic, a new political ethic, a new economic ethic, a new medical, educational, spiritual, and sexual ethic. This would require, it feels to me, the embracing of a new, collectively held idea about God, because even those who do not believe in God are affected and impacted by the eight out of ten humans who do, and whose idea about the Higher Power form the ethical basis of their choices and decisions.

Yes, considering and embracing a new, collectively held idea about God would be an experiment. We'd have to try it to see if it works. But I have this thought about it. Like the man who said the Earth revolves around the Sun, like the man who said germs exist and we need to sterilize against them, like the woman who insisted that jumping genes are *not* "junk DNA"...if we all decided to be Idea Heroes, we could turn the unbelievable into the believable.

Everything on Earth could change for the better virtually overnight if enough people were made aware of, allowed themselves to be open to, and embraced a New Definition of God, seeing the Higher Power as a self-conscious, self-aware, pure and undifferentiated energy which manifests as a feeling, and calling that feeling Pure Love.

Every human being is the spiritual and physical essence of Pure Love, and each person can express that energy by consciously engaging in the act of melding human emotions and Divine feelings, then projecting that energy it into the world in all the key moments of life.

There it is, in 100 words. The two paragraphs just above have summed up this entire text and provided us with what may just be the formula we have been looking for. You could, if you wanted to, find a way to share those 100 words with others. I understand that you'd have to be an Idea Hero to do it, but isn't that a perfect description of you?

It must be, or you would never have finished this book.

# AFTERWORD

Thank you for taking this journey with me. It is a source of inspiration for me to know that there are Idea Heroes everywhere, willing to look at and to explore, to poke and to prod, to challenge and even to change some old ideas and long-standing beliefs, and to see if there might not be a new way for us to proceed as a species heading into an uncertain future.

As part of our exploration, I invited you to play a bit with an idea, watching what thoughts ran through your mind about what a new belief system could look like if you were to start your own religion.

I'm curious about something now. As you considered this invitation, did it become clear to you that you really have some very concrete ideas about God? Or, conversely, did you experience that you have not thought about a Higher Power in such a specific way?

In this Afterword, I'd like to take a look now at some of what you may have come up with.

If you created your own religion, would it be pragmatic or dogmatic? That is, would it offer room for variances in on-the-ground application of your religion's messages as people grow in their understanding of life? Or would it require everyone to never vary on any principle or teaching in its canon? What do you think would work best to make the world a better place?

If you created your own religion, would it be inclusive or exclusive? That is, would it have space for people of differing ideas, of differing sexual orientations, of differing objectives in their spiritual and temporal life? Or would it require unwavering adherence to one way of life and one way only? What do you think would work best to make the world a better place?

If you created your own religion, would it declare that human beings are more than simply mammals, but are spiritual entities comprised of the foundational energy that sources all of life? Or would it announce that those who imagine themselves to be made of the same energy that sources life are instruments of evil? What do you think would work best to make the world a better place?

If you created your own religion, would it encourage toleration, acceptance, and love for those who choose not to belong to it? Or would it call for judgment, condemnation, and eternal punishment for everyone who does not embrace it? What do you think would work best to make the world a better place?

Finally, if you created your own religion, would it offer clear and unambiguous instructions on the nature and use of the Higher Power on which it would presumably be based? Or would it keep such formulas under wraps and out of reach for all but the most elite of its members? What do you think would work best to make the world a better place?

CRXO

Before we say goodbye, may I join now in the Thought Experiment?

I'd like to offer my responses to the questions that conclude Chapter 3.

See what you think of them.

If I were Chief Operating Officer of the Universe and could have things my way, here is the perspective I would bring after my 76 years on this planet, and given where I am in my evolutionary process:

Question #1: What does the Higher Power that some of us call "God" consist of? Is it an individual Spiritual Entity, something like a giant human being, with particular features that would be recognizable to, or may even resemble, our species?

My Answer: In my religion the element or aspect of Ultimate Reality that many people call God would not be described as a singular entity in the way that most people use the term. It would not be thought of as a huge, big, enormous "person", with human male or female physical characteristics, nor subject to human emotional experiences such as fear, anger, upset, approval, agreement, or need of any kind.

It would also not be defined as a force without self-awareness or consciousness (such as, for instance, the force of gravity). Rather, it would be defined as a self-conscious energy—an essential essence that is aware of Itself.

Think of this in the same way you might conceive of a thought. Your thought is not a person, it is an energy. But it is aware of itself. You can think about what you're thinking about. You can even have a thought about what you had a thought about what you had a thought about. You can go as far into this hall of mirrors with this as you wish. That comes close to what I mean when I say that God is a self-conscious energy that is aware of itself.

My religion would also teach that this energy is the Signature Vibration of the Cosmos, a particular and very specific frequency modulation that is both the originating and the organizing principle of everything, physical and non-physical. If I were speaking metaphorically, I might even call God "the Stem Cell of the Universe."

We have learned in relatively recent times that all living things contain what have been labeled stem cells. These are the earliest cells to form in any physical body. They have no specific characteristics, but rather, carry the coding for all possible characteristics. Eventually these undifferentiated cells differentiate, generating particular and specific elements of various body parts.

Using the power of analogy, God could be described as an essential essence which differentiates to become all that we call physical and metaphysical. Thus, God is the Source of Everything—and therefore, needs nothing.

My religion would teach, as well, that God is not just the source of everything, but the substance of everything. The Source and the Substance pretty well sums it up. This means that the idea that "separation" exists in the Universe would be a misunderstanding. We are neither separate from, nor other than, God, any more than a wave rolling on the surface of the ocean is separate from, or other than, the Ocean Itself. It is an arising *of* the ocean in a particular *form,* and it recedes back *into* the ocean when its individual expression is complete. The metaphor is a perfect description of our relationship with The Divine.

My religion would teach that God is the original Formless Form of this Essential Essence—which, as it is expressed and projected, generates a unique, singular, and specific effect, producing what sentient beings would call a "feeling."

Humans who have experienced themselves to have been touched by God have tried for millennia to portray or characterize this feeling. They have consistently settled on words which, taken together, could, I believe, be reduced to the single phrase I have chosen: Pure Love.

Speaking in fewer words, then, my religion would declare that God is Pure Love.

Question #2: What is its desire? If God needs nothing, does God even *have* desires?

My Proposed Answer: Yes. Needs and desires are not the same thing. My religion would teach that it is the desire of The Divine to continually create, as a means of experiencing in fullness the wonder of its Essential Essence. Yet life is not a *quid pro quo* arrangement. God does not create in order to get something back from that which God creates. God creates for the sheer joy of it. *That* is what God gets back. Sheer joy. So God does not have to demand something in return from that which God creates, nor does God decimate that which fails to give in return what God demands.

God experiences creation, I would offer, by placing within all sentient beings the power to collectively create their exterior reality, and to individually create their interior experience of all exterior events and circumstances, all through the exercise of Free Will.

The desire to create has been imbued in all sentient beings, who are never happier than when they are engaged in any creative activity, whether it is building something, trying something, producing something, inventing something, designing something, drawing something, painting something, composing something, cooking something, singing something, writing something—or simply rearranging the furniture in the living room or the flowers in a vase or the placement of the food in the refrigerator. Nothing gives us more satisfaction, nothing gives us more fulfillment, nothing gives us more pleasure than self-expression in any form.

It is precisely the same way with God.

An important aspect of this question about God's "desires" is this: Is it God's desire to punish souls with the everlasting damnation of eternal and indescribable suffering if God's mandates are disobeyed? Does God even have mandates (as opposed to desires)?

My religion would teach that the answer is "no" to both questions. It would offer that, given that God is Pure Love, God has neither a need nor a desire to punish anyone for not doing what God wants, because there is nothing that God wants or requires from us in order to be perfectly happy, any more than we would need or require something from a 3-year-old (much less a baby).

My religion would teach that we are babies in the eyes of God. And even if we weren't, God would have no need to "punish" us for behaviors that only those who do not fully understand Who They Are and Why They Are Here would exhibit. Even in human legal systems adults can be found "innocent by reason of insanity." If we are smart enough and compassionate enough to create such an awareness of the innocence of persons who are not capable of thinking straight, would not all the more God do so also?

Some other religions have taught that God will punish us for "offenses," even if those offenses keep changing from time and time, place to place, and culture to culture. But could it be that we are a young civilization still struggling to find itself and to decide what *we* think is "right" and "wrong," much less what *God* thinks?

To offer just one example, is exchanging sexual pleasure for money okay or not okay? Is it legal or illegal? Well, that depends on where you live, doesn't it? Brothels operate entirely legally in certain counties in Nevada in the United States. And, of course, Amsterdam, in The Netherlands, has been famous for its red-light district in a city where prostitution is not only legal, it is licensed, regulated and taxed as a revenue source by the government.

Other human activities as well have been deemed legal in one location or at one time in human history, and not in another, as humans continue to vary in their definition of what is Right and what is Wrong.

My religion would teach that God understands perfectly well the process by which a civilization in the cosmos evolves, and does not punish souls which participated in that process for behaviors they exhibited on the journey to their next understanding.

Question #3: What is the usefulness of the Higher Power? Can it even *be* "used"?

My Proposed Answer: My religion would share that the Higher Power has immense usefulness if it is utilized with intention and attention, purpose and focus. The religion would also share that God neither allows nor disallows, neither green-lights nor red-lights, specific occurrences or circumstances in the lives of sentient beings anywhere in the cosmos, but, as I said, gives all sentient beings Free Will to do so.

The religion would warn that, like all power, Free Will can be used in ways that produce intended or unintended, welcome or unwelcome, results as measured by human standards. The religion would teach how to use the Higher Power to manifest only *intended* events and circumstances—and even what humans would call miracles.

My religion would also teach that God's energy—that we have aptly called our Higher Power—was *meant* to be used, and that it has been placed at the disposal of all sentient beings in the cosmos *as the primary tool with which to create,* producing both their exterior collective reality and their interior individual reality.

❧

So how does all that sit with you? Any objections? Any concurrences? Perhaps you experience a little of both. Perhaps you can't embrace into the whole package, but there are a few elements with which you agree.

The trick here is to not allow the conversation to stop here.

For instance, one more thought could beneficially be expressed here. The idea that a person or a company or an organization or a religion expressing Pure Love needs, wants, requires, expects, and even hopes for nothing in return for its expression does not mean that nothing would be openly and joyously *accepted* if it were freely and joyously *offered* by the world in return.

Indeed, it is an *act* of Pure Love to *receive* life's gifts gracefully and graciously, for your receiving of the loving offering of others gives them the gift of expressing a part of themselves that brings them joy. It would be the antithesis of Pure Love if the love offering of another was something that givers of Pure Love felt they could not accept, because it was not needed or expected.

It is one thing to not expect anything in return for what you give, it is another thing to turn down what is offered. That stops the process of Divine Circulation. So by all means allow yourself to receive life's gifts as joyously as you give them.

It would be wonderful to keep discussing all of this, as putting our highest ideas firmly into place could change our lives and help change our world. You can find me at:

*www.NealeDonaldWalsch.com*

There, we can engage in ongoing exchanges on ways to understand and interact with God. As well, if you have a particular question you'd like to ask about any of the content here, or in the body of work I have produced relating to the publication of my previous *Conversations with God* series of books, you'll find me at the Ask Neale platform there regularly.

You can also find me at my Facebook page:

*https://www.facebook.com/NealeDonaldWalsch*

Feel free to stay in touch if it serves you to do so.

With Pure Love,

*Neale*

## IS IT MADE OF LOVE?

I don't know if my god is
the same as your god:

*Is it made of Love?*
Does it want for you
what *you* want for you?
Does it come to you
with hands opened,
asking nothing,
but ready for anything?

Does it whisper to you
of Light and of Stillness,
and point you toward
*any* of the paths
that will take you there?

Does it remind you
of your Seeing?
Does it remind you
of your Knowing?
Does it remind you
of the Gentlest Lover
ever you've dreamed,
caressing a weariness
from your heart?
Is it ever late?

Is it ever gone?

*Is it made of Love?*

© 2018 Em Claire
*emclairepoet.love*